MW00325465

TALES FROM THE

NASHVILLE PREDATORS
LOCKER ROOM

TALES FROM THE
NASHVILLE PREDATORS
LOCKER ROOM

A COLLECTION OF THE GREATEST
PREDATORS STORIES EVER TOLD

KRISTOPHER MARTEL

SPORTS
PUBLISHING

Library of Congress Cataloging-in-Publication Data is available on file.

Interior images by DMC Photography
Cover design by Tom Lau
Cover photo credit: Associated Press

ISBN: 978-1-68358-230-4
Ebook ISBN: 978-1-68358-231-1

Printed in the United States of America

For my mother.
I'll miss you every day.
I'm sorry you never got a chance
to read my finished book.

For my father.
Your love of sports stuck to me
from an early age. While I'm
sorry I never became a professional
athlete, I know you're proud of what I've
become instead.

For my children: Braylon, Kassie,
Hannah, and Zoey.
You are the four greatest bozos I could
have ever hoped to bring into this
world. I love you each so very, very much.

Finally, for my wife, Amanda.
You've sacrificed so much to allow me
to follow my dreams. I'll never be
able to thank you enough. Thank you
for your never-ending support and love.

CONTENTS

Acknowledgments

I would like to thank the entire Nashville Predators organization for their help in landing interviews with players, coaches, and management throughout the writing of this book.

I'd also like to thank the Montreal Canadiens, San Jose Sharks, Chicago Blackhawks, Detroit Red Wings, Arizona Coyotes, Washington Capitals, and Rockford Ice Hogs for assisting me with landing interviews as well.

I want to thank the fans who took time out of their busy schedules to email me about some of the moments highlighted in this book. It was a huge help!

A huge, massive thanks to Matt Skulley, who helped transcribe so many of my interviews. Without his help, I'd have been lost.

Introduction

I can't count the number of Nashville Predators games I've watched at Bridgestone Arena. Or the Sommet Center. Or Gaylord Entertainment Center. Or Nashville Arena. Whatever the name of the building is, I've seen hundreds of games. Numerous wins and losses from the stands and press row. Few, however, really stick out in my memory as games that I'll never forget.

Sure, games three and four from the first round of the 2004 playoffs will be there—match-ups against the rival Detroit Red Wings always provided plenty of memories, some of which will be highlighted in this book. A smattering of late comebacks during regular season games, including a mid-December night in 2010 against San Jose where Colin Wilson scored the game winner with less than three minutes remaining in regulation, also find space.

But one playoff game I doubt any Predators fan, or the players on the ice that night, will ever forget took place back on May 5, 2016. As Nashville battled travel fatigue and a 2–1 series deficit to the Sharks, it would take more than the normal 60 minutes to decide whether the Predators could even things up or not.

Three times previously had Nashville experienced an overtime game at home during the playoffs: game one of the Western Conference quarterfinals against the same Sharks in 2007, game three of the Western Conference semifinals against the Vancouver Canucks in 2011, and game one of the Western Conference quarterfinals against the Chicago Blackhawks in 2015—all three losses, two coming via double overtime.

Twenty minutes passed, then another 20. The Predators would find themselves in unfamiliar territory entering. Since 1980, this would be the 31st playoff game throughout the league to stretch into triple overtime or longer, but Nashville's first foray into anything past double overtime.

Passing the 110-minute mark, the halfway point into triple overtime, Nashville began to set things up in the offensive zone which led to the game-winning goal from Mike Fisher.

The longtime voice of the Predators, Pete Weber, with former assistant coach Brent Peterson beside him, had the call, followed by an elated directive for the fans:

"Go ape, everybody! Go ape! At 11:12 of the third overtime! The Predators have tied the series! It's a 4–3 win! HOLY COW!"

As the play unfolded, I was seated near the top of the press area above section 312. I had looked down for a moment to tweet something and looked back to the play right as the puck left Mattias Ekholm's stick, just prior to Fisher's rebound finding its way into the net.

When Fisher put the puck past Jones, I nearly broke the cardinal rule of "No Cheering in the Press Box." For one, it was the first time I had ever witnessed a home playoff win in overtime and, for the record, those are a thing of beauty to see up close. Nevertheless, it was nearing 2:00 a.m. Friday morning and I knew I'd now, at least, be able to sleep for a couple of hours.

Most Predators fans know what happened after that. Viktor Arvidsson would score an overtime winner just four nights later in game six to force Nashville's second-ever game seven, in back-to-back series, but nothing beats a triple-overtime winner unless it was to decide the Stanley Cup.

There are so many key moments surrounding this team that it was hard to nail down the best moments to fit into one book, but the organization continues to grow and define itself as Nashville approaches its 20th season. *Tales from the Nashville Predators Locker Room* shines a brighter light on some of the greatest moments, on and off the ice, in franchise history.

Have you ever wondered how David Poile works his trade magic? Or the conversation that started the trade between P.K. Subban and Shea Weber? What if a coach were to tell you that if you were scared, go get a dog? How would you respond? Were you inside the arena for the final TV timeout on April 3, 2008?

These are those stories. As best I could tell them, with the help of the players, coaches, management, and fans who gave me their insight along the way.

I can only hope you enjoy reading it as much as I enjoyed writing it!

– Kristopher Martel

Chapter One

Production Value: Behind the Scenes on Game Night

Most fans are oblivious to the day-to-day operations of a professional sports team, especially
that of game-night presentation. Brian Campbell, Director of Event Presentation for the Nashville Predators,
has been—in one way or another—a pivotal piece of the
organization since 1998 in terms of every facet of entertainment during a Predators game that doesn't involve
hockey.

Those early years saw the Preds do almost everything
they could to raise interest in not only the new NHL team
coming to Nashville, but hockey as a sport in general. For
Campbell, landing a job with the Predators may not have
been elegant, but it was a foot in the door to ultimately help-
ing them become a household name around Tennessee.

"I started in August of 1998. [The Predators] put an ad in the paper before they came to be the 'Street Team,'" says Campbell, who was hired alongside his college roommate at the time. "It was a way to promote the Preds before they got here. They hired us and said, 'you're going to go to bars and restaurants and pass out pucks and stickers,' and we were like what a perfect way to do anything. We get to go to a bar. We both like hockey. We get paid to do it, so we started with that.

"When the team came, we were the first members of the Kroger Nabisco Pepsi Puck Patrol. We did that for the first season and we were the first Energy Team. We didn't do it the second year; I ended up being a mascot assistant. I did help with appearances for Gnash and all that kind of stuff."

Campbell worked his way up from the lowest rung of the ladder, though truth be told there weren't many rungs to climb in the first years of the franchise. Whatever was asked of him, he took care of it. Sometimes that meant turning himself into the Preds' beloved mascot for an evening.

In the twenty years the Predators have been in existence, there have been but a few that have had the pleasure of donning the blue-skinned cartoon-esque sabretooth tiger outfit of Nashville's mascot, Gnash.

Of those few, only two have been Gnash full-time: Brett Rhinehardt, who left the team in 2001, and the current person portraying Gnash, who chooses to remain anonymous.

"I may or may not have ended up in the [Gnash] suit," Campbell recalled. "Our first Gnash [Brett Rhinehardt] blew out his knee and that's how I ended up in the suit. He came back for a limited time and then after that they came to me and asked me if I wanted to do it full time. I said no, and then they hired somebody else. After they hired him, I became a stage manager basically. A stage manager for the [event level], anything that went off and on the ice, that was what I was in control of.

"I did that for a number of years and just kind of worked games and events. They hired me on full-time a few years later. After the first strike, I went and worked for the [Tennessee] lottery for a year. I came back after the strike was over to a full-time position. After that, my boss Brian Schafer left and I went from being Game Operations Coordinator to Director of Event Presentation."

From the doors of Bridgestone Arena opening around 90 minutes prior to puck drop to announcing the evening's three stars of the game, the detail that goes into planning the entertainment for each Predators game is meticulous. While anthem singers and intermission bands are booked in advance, both practice to an empty arena in the half-hour leading up to the public being allowed into the building.

Campbell, who also oversees the live acts, spends the remaining time until puck drop running over the nightly schedule of events—down to the minute—with his game operations crew.

Most of what the operations crew addresses for each game is a manual process. The best comparison would be that of catering to a live studio audience for a hit television show. Campbell serves as the director of the show, making sure that everything runs without a hitch—to the best of his abilities.

This includes all skits involving Gnash; the videos and artwork that display on the Megatron during intermissions; and when the puck is frozen in-game, coordinating with Predators public address announcer Paul McCann to make sure the music is ready to go. In addition, Campbell personally oversees the control and operation of the goal horn button.

Yes, there's a button for the goal horn. One might be surprised to know that there comes a hefty fine if said button is pressed when a goal isn't scored, even if it was just an inadvertent slip of the finger. One might also be surprised to know that it bears zero resemblance to the famed "Easy" button.

"I blow the goal horn. It's not automatic," says Campbell. "It's a little red button and I have to watch [the play]. I knock on wood that I haven't made any mistakes over the years. It is a $10,000 fine if you prematurely blow the horn, too.

"I don't remember the exact game, but it was a Pittsburgh game because we call it 'The Penguin Rule.' They blew the goal horn, threw the lights and everything on a non-goal. Which some of the players stopped. During that same amount of time before they started over again, somebody actually did score. They said that goal was scored because of the distraction of everything and everything had stopped. Now for any premature goal celebration, there's a fine."

Unlike perhaps the NBA, where music and pre-recorded chants are played while the game is underway, the NHL does not have the same leniency. Being hundreds of feet away from the play, even with monitors to watch replays, Campbell and his staff must pay close attention as to not directly cause an audio or visual distraction while the on-ice action is underway.

"Any horns, bells, or whistles that go off? That distract the players? There's a fine for that," Campbell says. "You have to be very, very careful. You are supposed to wait for the referee to point to the net [indicating a goal], but there are a lot of times we don't see it or he's behind the net so we have to be careful with that."

Outside of the day-to-day activities, Campbell and his staff must plan and shoot the Megatron skits and videos on a yearly basis. Every fan has their own favorite skit or, in the same respect, one they aren't necessarily fond of.

None have ever been as polarizing as the "Monster Block," a short video of assorted Predators players, members of the dance team, and the goaltender waving his arms in the air to a repetitive tune loudly repeating its namesake. It's as entertaining as most other skits that Campbell and his crew execute on a nightly basis, but none can divide the fanbase—and sometimes the players themselves—much like the "Monster Block."

"We have two or three days during the preseason where we have to shoot [all skits and entertainment]. Some of the players are not as excited as others. And we pre-choose who we think would do a good job at certain things," said Campbell. "Some of the players will say no, some will be reluctant, and others, that we may not have picked, will be upset that we didn't pick them."

Prior to the 2017–18 season, Campbell and his crew were finishing up a marathon recording session with Predators defenseman Yannick Weber when the Swiss blueliner abruptly brought up the skit under his own accord.

"Wait. . . what about doing the 'Monster Block'?" said Weber, in an almost incredulous tone that he hadn't been asked previously.

"I'm sorry, you want to do what?" Campbell replied.

"I want to do the 'Monster Block'!"

This was a first for Campbell. No player had requested to participate in the "Monster Block" up to this point. Weber's request would not just include a truly active participant in the skit, but it would also open the door for others to request down the road.

Campbell had to make certain what he heard was accurate, because it was a first.

"Are you sure? You *want* to do the 'Monster Block'?"

With a level of euphoric excitement enveloping Weber, the defenseman confirmed his desire to Campbell and his team began to set the scene to record Weber's takes for the "Monster Block."

"Do you have the song?" asked Weber.

"I mean, we don't need the song," Campbell replied. "We just want you to wave your arms in the air."

Even knowing that, Campbell hastily pulled his phone from his pocket and began playing "Monster Block," with Weber immediately raising his hands and acting out the dance move.

"Yannick Weber wanted to do the 'Monster Block'," said Campbell. "There are others who do not. There are others that will do it and are a little more reluctant. There are others that get it and want to do it."

The idea of "Monster Block" was spawned during the 2016 Summer Olympics in Rio de Janeiro. Attempting to increase fan participation during volleyball events, the International Federation of Volleyball (FIVB) introduced that and a "Super Spike" segment that really resonated with the local fan base.

Those segments completely made sense in relation to Olympic volleyball, but would they transition well to ice hockey? Considering a goaltender wears a glove and blocker, often using the latter to help keep pucks away from the net, utilizing "Monster Block" makes sense. Nevertheless, having the Predators emulate its Olympic success and fashioning an in-game dance—much like the one that the St. Louis Blues incorporated for their powerplay—would prove to be a next-to-impossible task that was only met with levels of confusion instead of acceptance.

"I brought up the idea of 'Monster Block' during our annual creative session. Everyone seemed to be con-fused. There were like three people in the meeting that had watched women's volleyball," said Campbell. "In Brazil, they went nuts for [the 'Monster Block']. The DJ played it and everyone would dance along. I figured we could totally do this and if it doesn't work after a game or two, or if people just hate it, we'll stop doing it."

Campbell sent his thoughts over to Shane Blindert, Creative Content Producer for the Predators, and had him bring his vision to life. It wasn't until after the first time that Campbell utilized the "Monster Block" during a game would they receive any real criticism of it.

When the negativity came, it did so in the form of a simple five-word question: "What the hell was that?"

"I told them to just give it another game. If it doesn't work, great. If it does, even better," Campbell replied.

Over the course of twenty years, plenty of ideas will never see the light of day outside of creative meetings. However, it's the ones that are given the extra push that tend to be more well-received in the long run.

"The next game we did it, people started talking about it on Twitter and everywhere else. It became more polarizing than politics. It was like Trump/Clinton or 'Monster Block' Yay/'Monster Block' No. The next day, one of my bosses came to me and said we're done and we're not going to it anymore," Campbell recalled.

"The very next morning, that same boss came in and said, 'I have to eat my words. I came home from the game last night and my kids were at home and all they're doing is this "Monster Block" thing. I got to learn, and every-one else has to learn, that sometimes it's not about how we feel about things.' You have to take your own personal feelings out of it. There's a lot of things that we play or that other teams do that I don't like at all. You have to shoot for the majority instead of your own feelings."

Not everything that goes on behind the scenes is meant to make fans laugh, though.

Nashville annually hosts Hockey Fights Cancer nights each season in support of all individuals fighting cancer. One lucky individual receives the opportunity of a lifetime: being selected to participate in the Hockey Fights Cancer salute, which usually includes pregame festivities and a ceremonial puck drop before the game—where both captains oftentimes offer their hockey sticks as a gift alongside the ceremonial puck to the individual being honored.

Ten-year-old Predators fan Chase Donnell, who frequented games and practices, had been diagnosed before the start of the 2007–08 season with Burkitt's lymphoma, a rare and aggressive form of non-Hodgkin lymphoma. That season, he would be the one chosen for the annual Hockey Fights Cancer night.

Heartbreakingly, Donnell lost his fight with cancer before he would have a chance to enjoy the moment with his favorite team.

"It had been in the works for more than a week. We got a request from someone to have him on the bench and we had to go through different people in the [NHL], have Barry Trotz say yes and we were on the road at the time. We had to get all kinds of approvals to get him on the bench," says Campbell. "It took a while to get it all approved, but the story itself was pretty sad so we wanted to do something for him. The day it was approved, he passed away."

Now that everything had been approved by the coaching staff, the organization, and the league itself, Campbell and his staff were left in a bit of a bind. How could his crew continue with their plans now that the key figure involved had suddenly passed away? It was less than ideal for Campbell, who had yet to find himself in a situation like this throughout his career.

"We were asking ourselves what we were going to do," he says. "We ended up deciding to put his name on a jersey and put it behind the bench while we recognized his parents. I was kind of shocked that his parents wanted to come, but they were great."

Paul McCann, who has been Nashville's public address announcer since the 2006–07 season, was slated to tell Donnell's story as he was being honored during the pregame ceremony.

"It was honestly probably the most emotional thing I have ever been a part of," says Campbell.

"I was told about two days before," McCann recalled. "Those Hockey Fights Cancer reads are, quite honestly, they're the toughest thing I do in a year. Chase was a pretty cool kid. I had met him a few times and hearing that he had passed hit me hard."

The video of his tribute, which can be found on YouTube, lasts a little over 90 seconds. Halfway through, McCann slowly began to lose his composure, pausing for nearly 30 seconds before continuing with the end of the read.

"Chase was a pretty special kid," he says. "You could see even since then how many lives he's touched. He's got a special place in my heart."

✴   ✴   ✴   ✴

Through the highs and lows, one of Nashville's main focal points since joining the league in 1998 has been entertainment. Being a franchise placed in a non-traditional market, the Predators ownership and front office had to find ways to not only get people in the building, but bring them back for the next game.

"Our first five years or so, we gave away a house, we gave away a Corvette, we gave away everything we could, building things on entertainment first," Campbell says. "It was an expansion team in a non-traditional market. If you're going to spend $100 on a ticket, you better have some sort of other entertainment, because the hockey won't hold out. We kind of built things entertainment-first and hockey-second in hopes that eventually would equal out. It took a little longer than anyone expected, but not by too much."

As game operations have progressed over the last few seasons, and have easily become more technologically savvy in the same time span, Campbell is quick to remind anyone who asks that his business is one of first impressions.

"There's always somebody in the building that it's their first time [at a Predators game]," he says. "So no matter what you do, you have to keep that in mind. Even though some people have seen it, some people have not. Some people, this is their first game. You only have one chance to make your first impression and I think we've done a pretty good job. Once we get you in the building, you're hooked. It's a lot different than watching it on live TV.

"I've never really talked to anybody that's had a bad time. Win or lose, we want everyone to have a good time."

Campbell and his crew continually pride themselves on their work and their ability to produce one of the better in-arena shows across the league. It's one of the main reasons why ESPN listed Nashville as the number-one franchise in all of sports in October of 2017, noting that no team delivered to their fans more bang-for-the-buck than the Predators did.

While they may have to start competing with newer expansion teams like the Las Vegas Golden Knights in terms of pregame productions, especially when it comes time for the playoffs, Nashville remains the gold standard—no pun intended—across the league, and the game operations crew is a large reason why.

Chapter Two

George Parros or Borat?

I t's common that our brains are wired to see things that may not necessarily be there. Or, find comparisons where there isn't a comparison to be made. Sometimes those are justified, sometimes they're just downright wrong.

During his time with the Nashville Predators, forward Cody Hodgson often was told that he resembled noted actor Liev Schreiber—who is also known as noted hockey enforcer Ross "The Boss" Rhea in the *Goon* movie series. So striking was the resemblance that Hodgson would've likely had a role as a stunt double for Schreiber in the 2011 *Goon* movies, had it not been for his NHL career.

Often, these comparisons are innocuous in nature—meant as a compliment for most, or in the very least a stab at humor. Very rarely will a player have any issues with being compared to a Hollywood actor. Unless that actor happens to be Sacha Baron Cohen playing one of his many personalities.

Both teams, on any given night, tend to have at least one or two scratched players, who end up watching the game from the press box instead. Those players, for whatever reason they're scratched, take in the game from a distance and join the team in the locker room at the conclusion.

It's normally frowned upon for game operations staff to show scratched players sitting in the press box on the scoreboard during the game. Players can often be a healthy scratch, sometimes due to a coach's decision, and it's usually best practice to not make light of that situation. Predators Director of Event Presentation Brian Campbell, however, found himself making a simple mistake with what appeared to be just another fan in the stands in the midst of a game against the Anaheim Ducks during the 2006–07 season.

"Most of the scratched players tend to sit upstairs [in press row] or somewhere in that area," said Campbell. "We know not to show scratched players, especially from the other team. There's a lot of things that are planned on any given night, but a lot of things aren't. A lot of things are created on the fly. There's never a bad idea. If something is said to me, you may say it's stupid, but it may lead me to another idea and then another idea is generated from that and so on.

"Borat had just come out at the movies. We're panning the crowd and we say, 'oh my god, that guy looks like Borat!' And he did, he had that whole moustache and everything. So, somebody pulls a clip of Borat for the side-by-side look and I decided at the next whistle we were going to show this split-screen of this guy who looks like Borat and Borat and play the clip. So we hit the whistle, and this is in the lower bowl, we run it, the crowd loves it and they laugh. I didn't think anything of it. After the game, [Parros] went and complained. It turned out that he was the [Borat look-a-like]. I truly didn't know at the time."

Luckily, Campbell escaped any punishment because of it, however he learned a very important lesson that day: try not to compare an NHL enforcer to an actor who dons a mankini. You likely won't make many friends that way.

Chapter Three

The Thoughtful Alex Radulov

Players normally don't enter the offices on the corner of 6th Avenue and Broadway, opposite but parallel to the main guest entrance for Bridgestone Arena. It's an efficient separation: the employees do their job off the ice to run the business while the players do their job on the ice to execute the product.

When members of the production crew for the Predators need to grab video or comments from players, they'll head to a practice or an organized media gathering. It doesn't happen inside of Nashville's front office.

But this was no ordinary situation.

As he searched the cubicles for Brian Campbell, the Director of Event Presentation, forward Alex Radulov continued to call his name out until he finally found him. Interrupting his phone call, he brought up a personal request he wanted to see fulfilled.

"I'm on the phone and Alex Radulov walks up and says, 'I want to know who does bobbleheads. I want to have bobblehead done,'" said Campbell.

For all the promotions that Nashville has done throughout the years, releasing bobbleheads of their players hasn't been one that they've done that often. In fact, it took an overwhelming voice from the fans to inspire the last round of bobbleheads a couple of seasons ago—a set that included Seth Jones, Shea Weber, Roman Josi, Mike Fisher, James Neal, and Pekka Rinne.

"I wasn't exactly sure what he wanted so I asked him to repeat it," Campbell recalled.

"I want to make a bobblehead of me to send to my family," Radulov told Campbell.

The process of creating a bobblehead isn't cheap and isn't quick; it's a lengthy deal including taking pictures of the subject to make sure that the detail is accurate.

"We only order these in like 15 or 20 thousand," said Campbell.

"No, I want three bobbleheads. One for me and one for my mom and dad. I want to give to them for Christmas," replied Radulov.

Arguably, the cost of producing three custom-made bobbleheads in relation to the cost of manufacturing these in bulk for distribution may not necessarily be worth the trouble. But as a professional hockey player wanting a likeness of himself as a bobblehead for his parents as a keepsake? It's hard to say no.

"I told Alex ok and I'd see what I could do. We're going to need to take pictures and everything," Campbell said. "So for the next three weeks, Radulov would come up [and] ask if we were good on the bobbleheads."

Unfortunately, the bobbleheads would never see the light of day, as Campbell relayed that the finished product never came to fruition during Radulov's stay in Nashville.

It would have been interesting to see what an Alex Radulov bobblehead would have looked like and how it would have been received by the Predators fanbase. With the way that most of the fans have treated Radulov since his departure—largely in a respectable fashion, but he still gets booed like a normal visiting player—it's reasonable to believe that it could have been a great keepsake for those who collect Predators memorabilia.

After all, embattled as he was during his time with the Predators, forward Alex Radulov is arguably one of the more interesting players in Nashville's history.

Drafted 15th overall by the Predators in the 2004 NHL Entry Draft, Radulov was an incredibly promising prospect who was scoring at a near-unparalleled pace in the Quebec Major Junior Hockey League (QMJHL) for the Quebec Remparts. He would tie the team record for most points in a single game (7), set a record for the most consecutive games with a point streak at 50 (second in the entire QMJHL only to Mario Lemieux's 62 games), and finish the 2005–06 season with 152 points—a record still intact for the modern version of the Remparts, who were brought back to the QMJHL in 1997.

Radulov made his debut for Nashville on October 21, 2006, against the Vancouver Canucks, though he wouldn't record his first goal until the 26th of October against the San Jose Sharks.

During his time with the Predators, his career numbers were rather impressive: 47 goals, 55 assists in 154 games played—a not-too-shabby 0.66 points per game.

He may best be remembered for a couple of off-the-ice incidents—leaving the Predators prior to the 2008–09 season to play in the KHL and being suspended during

Alexander Radulov, along with Paul Gaustad and Roman Josi, preparing for a face-off against the Detroit Red Wings.

the second round of the 2011–12 Stanley Cup playoffs—but remains one of the more entertaining figures behind the scenes in Nashville.

Easy to talk to and nearly always approachable, Radulov was well-liked by the media and nary a negative word has been spoken about him from his former teammates. Defensemen Ryan Suter and Shea Weber both considered Radulov a close friend while in Nashville, as all three came up around the same time.

"He was a great teammate, a great friend," said Suter. "It was me, Rads, and Webs that were all kind of the same age and we all kind of hung out together. Kevin Klein was in that group. He was a fun guy and he loved to score goals and loved hockey and yeah, he was a good player."

Weber had the opportunity to not only have multiple stints with Radulov while in Nashville, but he played with

Andrei Kostitsyn, seen here during a game against the Detroit Red Wings, spent the final 19 games of his NHL career with the Predators.

Radulov once more after being traded to the Montreal Canadiens. While most fans tend to focus on the negative surrounding Radulov during his time with Nashville, his teammates looked past that and focused on the person.

"I think Alex still seems like a kid sometimes," said Weber. "He's got so much energy and he's so fun to be around, but we had a great relationship. He was a young kid. I was a young kid at the time. He loves hockey. He worked hard and he still works as hard as anyone out there."

Nevertheless, many fans will focus their disdain on the 2012 postseason, when Radulov and Andrei Kostitsyn

Radulov chasing a puck against Red Wings defenseman Ian White.

found themselves suspended for almost half of the series against the Arizona Coyotes, for being caught out past curfew.

There's no telling what Radulov and Kostitsyn would have done in those games or if Nashville would have continued to drop the series—and one of their most promising postseasons to that point—in five games to the Coyotes. There's no guarantee they would have advanced to the Western Conference Finals five seasons earlier than 2016–17.

What was guaranteed were Radulov's final days playing in a Nashville sweater, as he'd leave the team and head back to Russia after that season was over. After another four seasons in the KHL, Radulov would return to the NHL, playing stints with both the Canadiens and Dallas Stars.

Chapter Four

Setting the Bar—
On Nashville's
Rivalry against the
Detroit Red Wings

When the Predators entered the league for the 1998–99 season, the NHL went through a divisional restructuring to accommodate the newest franchise—dropping Nashville into the Central Division, where they joined the Chicago Blackhawks, St. Louis Blues, and defending Stanley Cup champion Detroit Red Wings.

Being a franchise placed in a non-traditional market as non-traditional as it can get in Nashville, the organization had to cater to some of its initial divisional foes and their fanbases to not only bring the crowds into the arena, but to possibly instill the sense of a developing rivalry into the players as well.

"I think that was one of our biggest rivals, especially at the time being in our division," said former Predators captain Shea Weber of the rivalry with Detroit. "Playing them eight times a year and knowing that they were such a historic franchise, you know, it's like a measuring stick. We'd always try and measure ourselves up to them with the success they'd had and the Stanley Cups they'd won.

"It was definitely not difficult to get up for those games, and I think by no means were they easy games, either. I think they were physical and intense and I think the fans loved those games as much as we did."

Building a rivalry takes time. It's not going to happen the first night two teams face each other. With the attitude the Predators coaching staff brought when they played the Red Wings and the influx of northern transplants that worked in the auto plants around Nashville, it wasn't going to take very long.

Former Predators head coach Barry Trotz understood this. When it came to modelling his organization, he wanted to do it the right way and build it to the greatest standard possible. At the time, the Red Wings provided a perfect example.

Detroit had won back-to-back Stanley Cup championships entering Nashville's first season, compiling 154 wins over the previous three years. Their roster? A who's who among future Hall of Fame players: Steve Yzerman, Brendan Shanahan, Igor Larionov, Sergei Fedorov, Nicklas Lidstrom, Slava Fetisov, and more.

"Detroit was the gold-standard for a lot of years," said Trotz. "They were the big-money team. They were spending $72 million while we were spending $13 [million]. They were the gold-standard, they won a lot of games, they won some Cups. They had the Who's Who.

At one time, I think I counted they had eight or nine future Hall of Famers on their bench. Because they were so good, I always looked at Detroit as the gold-standard. They made us better by being in our division."

"We always called them 'Big Brother' and we knew we had to kick Big Brother's butt, sooner or later, in order to get anywhere and go anywhere," said Terry Crisp, currently an analyst for FOX Sports Tennessee as well as a Stanley Cup-winning coach and player. "So every game we played with Detroit was a measuring stick, and they were ours. I can remember the first time we beat them ever and we were like we just won the Stanley Cup. We're like, hell, we got the Stanley Cup beat now, we just beat Detroit! Well, it took a few games later to duplicate it."

The Predators and Red Wings would play each other a minimum of five times a year up until Detroit shuffled over to the Eastern Conference for the start of the 2013–14 season. Through the first five seasons of Nashville's history, the Predators recorded a total of six wins over the Red Wings.

Six wins in 27 games. Only one of those six wins came inside Joe Louis Arena.

It wasn't the most shocking of things to happen to the Predators in their first handful of seasons. The wins weren't flowing in quickly for the Predators while they were still building their team. It took ample time before Nashville largely found itself competitive against the Red Wings, and many other opponents, on a year-to-year basis.

"We had to play them more probably than anyone else, it seemed like," said Trotz. "We played them in preseason, we played them in the regular season, and we started playing them in the playoffs."

The Predators would win their second-ever game against Detroit 5–3 on December 23, 1998. A three-goal period for Nashville would doom the Red Wings, as both

Cliff Ronning and Scott Walker would record two-goal nights to give the Preds their third two-game winning streak of the season—which they'd continue three nights later against the Washington Capitals, marking the first-ever three-game winning streak for the franchise.

They wouldn't beat the Red Wings again until December 4, 1999—four games and nearly a full calendar year later. The 4–1 victory over Detroit would snap a seven-game losing streak for Nashville in a season where it had only won 28 games—tied for the third-worst season in team history (only the 1998–99 and 2001–02 teams were statistically worse).

"I always relate this to Detroit and the Predators," said Crisp. "When I was coaching out West in Calgary against Edmonton, Cliff Fletcher built the Calgary Flames to beat the Edmonton Oilers. Not the other 29 teams, we didn't worry about them because we knew full well that the Stanley Cup ran through Edmonton, and if we were ever going to get at it, we had to knock off Edmonton. That was our feeling with Detroit. We felt that once we could beat them, we could move on from there."

"For us being a new team, they were the team to beat," retired Predators forward Scott Hartnell said. "You could go down the list of their guys who are in the Hall of Fame or multiple Stanley Cup winners. Emotions always ran high.

"We were in a different place than they were: an expansion team where our top guy made a million or two dollars and Brett Hull, [Chris] Chelios, and those guys were making a lot. We were competitive. Our identity was totally different than theirs. Still, every night it was a game. It was fun being the underdog."

As the Predators grew off and on the ice during the franchise's inaugrual years, they continued to build their roster through free agency in the draft—attempting to catch Detroit in the process, one way or the other.

Nashville would compile a 6–16–2 record (plus three ties) in its first five seasons against the Red Wings. It wasn't until the 2003–04 season that competition between the two teams would start to escalate.

After winning three of their first four games, the Predators had dropped four straight coming into an October 23rd meeting against Detroit—the first of seven divisional meetings between the two teams that year and one of two meetings separated by only nine days.

The Red Wings weren't off to a great start either, losing four of six after starting the season with three straight wins.

Forwards Jeremy Stevenson and Darren McCarty would have words to start the game and it wouldn't take but 23 seconds from the time the puck dropped to gloves being shaken free and fists flying between the two.

It was the first of nine fights that evening.

Through the first 40 minutes between both teams, 72 penalty minutes had already been dished out—and that wouldn't even be half of the final total.

When it came time to drop the puck for the third period, all hell was ready to break loose.

Halfway into the final frame, Steve Yzerman, Kirk Maltby, and Scott Walker would be tossed from the game. Brendan Shanahan, Mathieu Dandenault, Adam Hall, Jeremy Stevenson, Darren McCarty, and Jamie Allison would all follow.

Whatever had burrowed itself under Detroit's skin that night seemingly brought out the best in the Predators. It was the message Nashville had wanted to send to the Red Wings for the previous five seasons, that they were in the division for the long haul and they were going to compete with Detroit every single night.

Most importantly, though, it was that Nashville would no longer be pushed around. They were going to hold their own against any team in the NHL—from the Atlanta Thrashers to the active dynasties like the Red Wings.

"What it told me was, and I know from when I played, that when you come back in the dressing room after one of those, you're high-fiving each other," said Crisp. "You got eight stitches cut above your eyebrow. You got a nose bent. You're missing a tooth but yeah! Yeah, baby! We were there, we stood up in the schoolyard, and they know full well that we're going to bite them on the ankle next time again, too!"

The Predators would finish that season headed to the playoffs for the first time in franchise history. Waiting for them were the Red Wings, Nashville's official welcome wagon to the NHL's second season.

It was a new experience for the Predators, facing off against the same team for up to seven straight games. Only a handful of players on the team had previous experience in the playoffs and going up against the number one-seeded Red Wings was a tall task for any team.

If the start of game one was any indication of how Nashville had prepared themselves to play against Detroit, the Predators certainly didn't appear to be an inexperienced bunch against the President's Trophy-winning Red Wings.

Sixteen seconds into the game, Predators captain Greg Johnson would corral the puck behind the net of Detroit goaltender Manny Legace before sending a centering feed to forward Adam Hall. Hall, in turn, wired one to a stunned Legace, who buried the subsequent rebound that fluttered directly to the right of his pads.

Nashville's first playoff goal in franchise history would come at the expense of Detroit at Joe Lewis Arena 16 seconds into the game. You couldn't have scripted a better start for the Predators.

Seventy-four seconds after that, Steve Sullivan would have a chance to cash-in on Nashville's first play-off penalty shot—yet fired it high and wide over Legace's glove. The Preds had come out of the gate blazing hot, nearly taking a 2–0 lead less than two minutes into the game and holding Detroit to one shot over the first seven minutes.

Not only were the Predators attacking Detroit back into their own zone, but goaltender Tomas Vokoun was equally lights out during the first 40 minutes of the post-season, stopping all 18 shots from the Red Wings.

What Nashville had yet to learn in its history was that 40 minutes of solid hockey wouldn't nearly cut it in the playoffs; it takes a full 60 and sometimes more.

Thirty-seven seconds into the third period, Kris Draper cut through Predators defensemen Mark Eaton and Brad Bombardir and fired a puck straight through the five-hole of Vokoun to tie the game at one.

The Red Wings were awake. Over the next four minutes, Detroit would pepper the Preds in their own end before Tomas Holmstrom redirected a Mathieu Schneider shot from the point past a screened Vokoun, giving the Wings their first lead of the game.

Detroit ended up taking game one by a final of 3–1, a game where Nashville dominated the majority but couldn't find a way to finish off a team that was built for moments like that.

"That's why they're former Stanley Cup champions," said Sullivan after the game. "They know they can get the job done, it's just a matter of time. We just have to do a little better of a job trying to hold on a little harder."

A stronger defensive effort from both teams in game two led to a 1–1 game going into the third period. With the possibilities of overtime looming for both teams as they remained tied going into the final five minutes of regulation, whoever committed the next mistake would surely regret it.

Unfortunately for the Predators, fate wouldn't be on their side. It all began to fall apart when Chelios passed the puck forward through the neutral zone toward Nashville's end, and Hartnell slid through and delivered a crushing blow after the fact—putting Hartnell in the box for interference with 3:25 left on the clock.

Forty seconds later, the Red Wings took a 2–1 lead and held on for a 2–0 series lead against the Predators. Again, the Preds were their own worst enemy.

As the series shifted back to Nashville, Predators fans finally got to witness NHL playoff hockey in their city—making sure they pulled out every stop in the process. There may have been louder moments to date, but up until then the building had never shaken as it had on that cool spring day in Nashville.

The energy helped the Predators earn their first playoff victory in franchise history, beating Detroit 3–1 in front of a sell-out crowd at the Gaylord Entertainment Center—highlighted by both David Legwand's short-handed goal and Adam Hall's regular strength marker coming in the final two minutes of the first period.

Continuing their progress from game three, the Predators blanked Detroit 3–0 in game four to even the series—seeing coach Dave Lewis pulling Legace during the game in favor of long-time NHL journeyman Curtis Joseph, who got the start for the pivotal game five.

Whether it was the goaltending change or the shock that the Predators had delivered to Detroit's system, the Red Wings had had enough. Back in the comfort of the Joe Lewis Arena, Detroit grabbed a 3–2 series lead with a dominating 4–1 win in game five.

Nashville would eventually drop their playoff series that year against Detroit in six games as well as in

2007–08. Both times saw the Predators lose the first two games at Joe Louis Arena, before tying the series at home and then losing games five and six.

"The Joe was a tough place to play in, but it was a fun place to play because of all the history," said Weber. "I think home ice advantage is a big deal in the playoffs, especially when you've got great fans behind you and it's always tough playing against a team that's got so much experience in the playoffs and having gone through it before and seen it and done it."

Eight years after their inaugural playoff series against the Red Wings, and one season after winning their first playoff series in franchise history, the Predators would get their third crack at Detroit in what would be one of Nashville's most entertaining match-ups. This time, they'd have a decided advantage with home ice for the first round.

"It was huge," Weber noted. "The energy levels and excitement that the fans bring into every game really gives the guys a little extra boost and momentum to play those games and ultimately helps you use that to win games."

The teams split the first two games of the series at Bridgestone Arena, leaving Nashville with the tall task of having to win at least one of the two games back in Detroit in order to regain the home-ice advantage that Detroit had won away after game two.

Nobody could have predicted that the Predators would travel up to Detroit and sweep both games at Joe Lewis Arena to head back to Nashville with a 3–1 series lead for a potential series-clinching game five.

The Predators were on the cusp of finally putting their biggest rival in the rearview mirror. And it only took them nearly fifteen years to do so.

Pekka Rinne, Nashville's all-time leader in playoff victories as of 2018, helped lead the Predators to their first playoff series win over Detroit.

With the Red Wings on the ropes, Nashville made every effort to put them away early in the contest, but to no avail. Every chance, every shot, Detroit had a counter for it. They weren't going to go away that easily.

With the teams tied at one going into the third period, game five had the potential to be an absolute classic.

Detroit was able to win the opening face-off of the period, but the Predators immediately re-gained possession. Alexander Radulov drove the puck into the zone and passed it off to Gabriel Bourque, who was streaking toward the net immediately to his right. With Bourque covered by two defensemen, the puck was poked back to a waiting David Legwand, who used the dual-defensive screen on goaltender Jimmy Howard to laser the puck into the net 13 seconds into the third period.

With the roof nearly blown off the building, Nashville had a 2–1 lead in the game that they'd never relinquish. The Predators finished the game with the same score and

Andrei Kostitsyn shoots a puck past Red Wings goaltender Joey MacDonald as forward David Legwand looks on.

took the series four games to one. Three times Nashville had faced off against their chief rival, but only the final time would they make it over the hump and see the proverbial torch passed off from "big brother" to "little brother."

Even with Detroit now in the Eastern Conference, the Predators haven't forgotten about their roots—especially with their Original Six rival showing up only twice a year.

Nashville's rivalries with the Chicago Blackhawks and Anaheim Ducks haven't had the same type of raw passion that the first years of the franchise produced against Detroit. Yet, the Predators continue to see old rivalries end and new rivalries form.

These days, the Predators have become the team that other franchises modeled themselves after. In their own division, the Winnipeg Jets and Colorado Avalanche looked at how the Predators were built and slowly started to shape their rosters in the same fashion. The 2017–18 playoffs saw Nashville face off against both teams in the first and second round, respectively, with the Avalanche being knocked out in six games while Winnipeg got the best of the Preds in seven.

There's no question that the Predators may be the gold-standard in the Central Division now, taking the mantle from both the Blues and Blackhawks; however, it all started with their desire to be like the Red Wings. Luckily for Nashville, it was a solid franchise to chase over the first fifteen years of the franchise.

Chapter Five

The Jiri Fischer Incident

Over the course of an 82-game season, players tend to see the best and worst of life happen on the ice. Whether it's a three-goal comeback victory in overtime on the road or a poorly-officiated contest ending with a controversial decision, nothing comes as a shock to most who play sports at a professional level.

We use the words "life or death" rather loosely in life. Got an emergency at work? "It's life or death, give me a call." Out of milk for your children? "Life or death." When something truly happens that is a life or death situation, how do we react? Shock, surprise, inability to process it?

November 21, 2005, was just another Monday for the Predators. Nashville had flown into Detroit after their loss to Minnesota on Friday night, which halted a four-game winning streak. They were already off to the best start in franchise history: eight straight wins to start the year and a combined record of 12–3–3 going into Monday's game against the Red Wings.

Stepping out into a cold, windy November day in the Motor City, the Predators players and coaches prepped for the game as they did any other one. Morning skate, meetings, and back to the hotel—nothing was out of the ordinary.

Day turned to night, and Joe Lewis Arena—the home of the Red Wings from 1979 until 2017—filled with the normal, fiery Red Wings fanbase. The second game in Nashville's three-game road-trip was underway.

As both teams battled during the first period, the Predators gained the upper hand midway through as captain Greg Johnson scored the first goal 11:28 in. Yet just one minute later, tragedy struck.

Predators forward Scott Hartnell remembers the scene vividly. Something was wrong; it just didn't immediately process at first. As the puck slid through the defensive zone, Hartnell continued to attack the puck and re-gain possession for Nashville.

Until his eyes darted ahead and more Detroit players started filling the ice.

"I was on the ice and we were in the defensive zone," Hartnell recalled. "The next thing you know I looked up and all I can see is four or five [Red Wings] players skating towards the Zamboni entrance. Your first thought was that there were too many men, or that kind of stuff because you're involved in the game."

As confusion mounted both on and off the ice, players from both teams grew increasingly aware that this wasn't any ordinary stoppage of play. Nashville's players stood up at the bench and looked down towards their counterparts; something was dreadfully wrong for the home team.

Panic set in.

Red Wings players who were on the bench recognized one of their teammates had collapsed close to the bench door, directly in front of the tunnel leading back to the dressing room. As Hartnell approached and looked on, Detroit head coach Mike Babcock uncharacteristically jumped on top of the bench and screamed toward the Zamboni tunnel.

"Help! Help!"

The guard in charge of security standing directly inside the tunnel frantically yelled and waved toward Red Wings doctors, who ran toward the bench to see what had happened.

"We knew it was bad," said Terry Crisp, who was the television color analyst for the Predators at the time. "We knew that when the players looked at him, the players start and then they see the looks and the doctors are coming down, but the one thing that we were told and taught was to not assume because he has relatives listening. Don't try to guess what happened.

"So we laid off of what really was going to happen to him, didn't know until later on, but when you know both teams go deathly quiet out there, and both teams are standing quietly at their benches, it's serious. It's not just another six stitches or another whatever, and that was a scary, scary moment."

"Some of the guys kept playing," said Chris Mason, former Predators goaltender and current television color analyst. "It happened at different times where some of them realized something was wrong. I was on the bench and I noticed the guys on the ice and the bench started looking over at [Detroit's] bench. I look over to their bench and you can just see the panic on their players' faces. They had players waving down the tunnel just to get someone out quickly. Nobody really knew what happened."

Hunched over at the bench, Red Wings forward Jiri Fischer was in the midst of a heart attack—unbeknownst to the players and coaches surrounding him—all but ending his career. The chaos grew as the seconds passed.

And then the unthinkable happened—Fischer's heart stopped.

"You see players get hurt, but this one was different," said former Predators head coach Barry Trotz. "For a couple of moments, he was a lifeless body lying on the bench."

"I ended up taking a little skate by their bench," Hartnell added. "Everyone was standing there just to see what happened and who it was. He looked as lifeless as could be."

While doctors and technicians continued to work on Fischer, both teams had poured onto the ice as players and coaches comforted one another as the life of one of their companions hung in the balance.

As some personnel looked on from the bench at the situation unfolding, doctors and medical technicians quickly began CPR and used an AED—Automated External Defibrillator—to bring Fischer back to.

"Right away, as soon as we were aware as to what was going on, we got medical help right away," said Babcock to media after. "They started doing CPR on him. His heart had stopped and there was no pulse, but they hooked up the auto defibrillator and they shocked him. They continued with the CPR. Our medical staff did a phenomenal job."

Red Wings captain Steve Yzerman and center Kris Draper quickly skated toward the Zamboni entrance, where a stretcher was slowly making its way toward the bench. Intercepting it, the two Detroit players hastily brought it over to medical personnel who were continuing to work on Fischer.

"You see the guy laying there and the doctors working, doing what they're doing," said Yzerman. "You're obviously concerned. You fear for the guy's life."

"The ref came over and said, 'We're going to go in the dressing room. Fischer collapsed.' So we went in the dressing room," Mason said. "Everyone got off the ice and we're sitting in the dressing room. We got an update and Trotzy came in and told us what happened. I remember Tomas Vokoun, Marek Zidlicky, and Martin Erat all knew and had a relationship with Jiri Fischer. They were emotionally distraught and there were tears, everything like that. It was just dead silence in there."

After use of a defibrillator at the bench and stabilizing him, Fischer was transported to a nearby hospital. With his status unknown, the officials and the league made the decision to postpone the contest to a later date—when Nashville would ultimately win 3–2, having maintained their one-goal advantage from the postponed game.

"We had never gone through something like this," said Shanahan. "It was shocking and scary. Thank goodness our doctors were nearby and sit right by our bench and were on the scene right away."

For as physical as the sport of hockey is, it's surprising that serious medical issues aren't more common across the NHL. Teams, and the NHL in general, have doctors on staff and expert medical professionals on-call when issues like this arise.

Even though medical personnel saved Fischer's life, his hockey career ended that night in Detroit. He wouldn't play another game professionally and would be medically forced to retire at the end of the 2006–07 season. Fischer continues to work for the Red Wings to this day, as their Director of Player Evaluation.

"You didn't know if he was going to live or die," noted Hartnell. "As crazy as this sounds, this is just a game. It would have been tough to go on and play the rest of that game not knowing how he was at the hospital."

Mason echoed Hartnell's sentiments. "You get so consumed in hockey," he said. "When you're a hockey player, everything you do revolves around hockey: what you eat, how you train, when you sleep. Every single thing you do revolves around hockey. Events like that give you that realization that it's just a game. Life's the most important thing. It's too bad sometimes that that's what it takes. It's nice that it worked out after that, but it's an eye-opener."

"When they said 'Hey, we're just calling the game off,' it was the right thing to do," Trotz said. "We're entertainers, nothing more. We don't cure cancer. We don't educate people a whole lot. We're just entertainers. When you get an opportunity to be in that situation, you realize how precious life is and how small our game really is."

Chapter Six

Leaving for Minnesota

Outside of a player like Jimmy Vesey spurning a Predators organization that drafted him out of college to sign with the New York Rangers, there may be no better example of heartbreak than that of defenseman Ryan Suter.

Drafted seventh overall in the epic 2003 NHL Entry Draft held in Nashville, the same one that saw the Predators grab Kevin Klein and Shea Weber, Suter spent the next nine years as a member of the Predators—becoming a mainstay on the NHL roster in 2005 and never looking back.

With Suter approaching the end of his final restricted free agent contract with Nashville after the 2012 season, he, Weber, and Pekka Rinne would all be unrestricted free agents at the end of the year—leaving the Predators in a bit of a pickle: could they re-sign all three to new contracts or would they end up losing one or more of the three most impactful players on their roster?

For Nashville, at the time, it wasn't a monetary issue. The Predators had the resources to make sure all three stars were locked into long-term contracts. The bigger question was whether all three *wanted* to be with Nashville long term.

They were a franchise on the rise. The hiring of both CEO Jeff Cogen and COO Sean Henry back in 2010 sparked a new flame in the organization. Bridgestone Arena became a top destination across North America, with the Predators being their centerpiece.

Nashville's on-ice product had also drastically improved, winning 95 games over the previous two seasons and making it as far as the second round of the playoffs in both—a far cry from a team that had never won a playoff series prior to the 2010–11 season.

All three were central to Nashville's plans of making it back to the second round of the playoffs—and beyond—going forward. It was critical that general manager David Poile find a way to keep all three with the organization.

One year prior during the summer of 2011, Poile tipped his hand slightly, sending Cody Franson—who would be a free agent the next summer, much like Suter—to the Toronto Maple Leafs for Brett Lebda and Robert Slaney, but also removing the final two seasons of injured forward Matthew Lombardi's three-year, $10.5 million contract.

Outside of Nashville, most could see exactly what Poile was doing: shredding cap space to make way for re-signing Rinne, Suter, and Weber.

*   *   *   *

Rinne was the first to lock in with the Predators, signing a seven-year, $49 million contract in November 2011. Poile's ability to sign Rinne a month into the regular season gave him ample time to finalize deals with both Suter and Weber.

In the first two months of the season, Nashville finished 11–9–4 by the end of November. After that the team kicked it into high gear.

Suter had a career year, posting personal bests in assists and points with 39 and 46, respectively. It helped the Predators fly through the final four months of the season with a 37–17–4 record, ending the year at 48–26–8—104 points, which would be five behind the St. Louis Blues for the Central Division crown and giving them a spot as host to the Detroit Red Wings in the first round of the playoffs.

As the season wound down, the playoffs came and went without either of Nashville's top two defensemen signing extensions with the team—much to the fear of fans and management alike.

Both blueliners had lauded Nashville as a city and the Predators organization, both noting their desire to stay long-term.

Poile and Suter, along with Suter's agent Neil Sheehy, spoke in November—around the time of Rinne's signing—about what the defenseman's plans were regarding the Predators.

"[Suter] told me today that our offer was 'substantial' but that it was not about the money," Poile told reporters via a conference call. "So I said, 'Then I don't know why you're not re-signing with us.' And he told me it was for family reasons. That's where the disappointment comes in. The disappointing part is that's not what we talked about all year long. I think we met

Ryan's desires on every front so today is very, very disappointing.

"I was looking at all my notes from yesterday and [Suter] had said in November that he's not going anywhere else. He is signing with the Nashville Predators. That's a quote," Poile said.

Promises aside, Suter signed a 13-year, $98 million-dollar deal with the Minnesota Wild on July 4, 2012, sending Predators fans in a tizzy and prompting Poile to address the media about what his previous discussions with Suter and his agent entailed. It's probably one of only a handful of times Poile's emotions have clearly boiled over as he met with media members.

Looking back, there was a lesson to be learned, and maybe it's helped how Poile's shaped the Predators since. It certainly taught him that even a veteran in this business can make a rookie mistake from time to time.

"I could be in denial when I'm asked the question because, you know, I took him on face value," said Poile. "We did make the playoffs that year and if we would've traded him, you could make the case that we wouldn't have made the playoffs. I go over that all the time. There's certainly a lesson to be learned there. I thought we had a good relationship.

"I probably should have been more forceful to get commitments or have commitments with both Suter and Weber at an earlier time, but I didn't and, again, it's just one side of the story. You know, they maybe had a different agenda, I don't know, maybe just Suter getting close to home, but I think there was other teams involved and it still was about money."

The loss of Suter was a deep and stinging blow to both Poile and the Predators franchise. There were no indications what Weber would be doing in the very near future, whether he would work out a new deal with Nashville or follow suit with the now-departed Suter. What was clear, though, was the Preds had lost an eight-year veteran of their defensive group.

One year after Suter and Poile went through their nasty divorce, both had a chance to mend the seemingly broken bridge—as the two would chat after Nashville's morning skate prior to a January 22, 2013 meeting between the Predators and Wild.

"He's just a classy guy," Suter said, speaking to media about the meeting afterwards. "I have a lot of respect for him. He's given me a lot of opportunities. I'll always respect him and appreciate him."

"If I was emotional, I don't make any apologies for that. It was disappointing the way it turned out for us," Poile said in an interview with the *Tennessean* newspaper later. "I have nothing bad to say about Ryan. He was a terrific player for us."

Suter, to this day, continues to proclaim that he made Poile 100 percent aware of his intentions to hit free agency during the summer of 2012.

"I told David Poile that, right from the start, right before the All-Star Game, I'm going to wait until July 1st and see what's out there," Suter said, with a certain level of dominance in his voice. "I was straight up-front with him right from the start and I guess the rest is history.

"I told everyone I was like, 'hey, I want to see what my options are and I'm going to make the best decision for my family.' I was up-front with everyone right from the start."

Predators fans have yet to entirely forgive Suter for leaving the team. Years after he left the organization, a loud contingent of the arena would boo his name when announced for starting line-ups, boo his name whenever he touched the puck, and cheer wildly if Suter were hit by a Predators player or if he found himself in the penalty box.

This has all occurred despite the fact that Suter's decision was largely swayed by what was best for his family.

"I think that that was the biggest thing," said Suter. "My wife was from Minnesota and to be three and a half hours away from your hometown and to be in a market like Minnesota? I grew up playing, skating outside on the outdoor rinks and I wanted my son, my kids to experience that same thing."

It also gave Suter the opportunity to spend more time with his parents. His father, Bob Suter—a member of the 1980 United States "Miracle on Ice" team—would pass away only two years later.

"He was everything," Suter said about his father. "I'd call him after the games and we wouldn't talk that much about hockey but if I had questions, I'd ask him. He would give me his opinion on something if I asked him, but he was always there for my family and for me.

"With the decision, he basically told me to do what's best for myself and whatever I thought. We would talk about different teams and different areas and things like that, but he was pretty hands-off with that."

As the years pass, Suter's grown out of any hurt feelings when it comes to the boos that rain down on him in Nashville. In fact, it's become a part of what drives his teammates during those games.

"I think it's kind of funny," said Suter. "I think other people were trying to keep [leaving the Predators] on the down-low. I think that's what made me out to be a bad person. I have a lot of great memories here. I have a lot of respect for the organization and the fans. I loved it here. The booing thing, it doesn't bother me. [My teammates] actually get a little more fired up, so I like it."

Shea Weber, along with Ryan Suter, spent the majority of their playing time in Nashville on the same defensive pairing.

If Predators fans knew that booing Suter gave his teammates an energy boost, perhaps they might be inclined to change their tone.

As for Weber, he has a slightly different perspective than most Preds fans.

"If [Suter] felt he wasn't getting treated how he saw himself with the Predators or whatever the reason may be, maybe he just wanted to move closer to home for his family to be closer to family," said Weber. "It's something that free agency allows players to do, so I don't think anyone was mad at him for that. I think we would have loved to keep him because he's a great defenseman, still is a great defenseman, so it would have been nice to keep him along with all the other guys that Nashville's grown over the years, but those are the way things work sometimes and things change."

Chapter Seven

What to Do When $110 Million Comes Looking for You

Predators general manager David Poile knew it was possible for a different team to try and offer sheet a player like Shea Weber. He just had no clue as to why his counterparts in Philadelphia would even try it at this point.

Ryan Suter had just signed a massive deal with the Minnesota Wild, departing Nashville and drawing the ire of Poile—who had thought he'd be able to get a deal done with Suter to keep him with the Predators.

Nashville had again seemingly lost one of their key defensemen to free agency, this time with Shea Weber, owner of one of the hardest shots in the entire NHL and top blueliner for the Preds—the last of the three major cogs to the well-oiled machine that Nashville was.

"We didn't have a deal done on July 1, you knew it was a nervous time and the Suter thing, it almost comes back to back," Poile said, recalling the two hectic weeks back in the summer of 2012. "Obviously, it's a very unknowing time in our franchise. Did I think, again, that we're going to sit down and talk and make a deal? Yes, but [Weber] and his agents had a different plan."

Signing an offer sheet with the Flyers two weeks to the day after Suter had left the organization, Weber's deal was massive: fourteen years, $110 million dollars—$68 million of which was guaranteed over the course of the first six years of the contract.

The problem, there? Nashville was going to match it one way or another. They weren't prepared to lose both of their star defensemen in the first two weeks of free agency.

"[Offer sheets] are a tool that the players have negotiated for that they have," said Poile. "Not all but almost every offer sheet has been matched and I could say the same thing to Philadelphia. We're just going to match it. I mean, we just lost Suter. This is a no-brainer, so I didn't appreciate them doing that."

As he spoke to Flyers management prior to the offer sheet being announced, Poile said he didn't mince words for what he felt was a less-than-ideal situation for everyone.

"I'm 100 percent confident our ownership is going to match it," said Poile. "I don't even know why you're doing this because it's not logical on your end."

By Poile's account, the conversation grew more heated as the topic of money became more of the focal point.

"You're costing us money," replied Poile. "This is what we would've paid him in the end. We just have to pay a little bit more now so we'll just go to the bank and borrow it. So we're just paying interest. That's all."

He was furious. Poile had worked in this business as a general manager for over thirty years. He had lost Scott Stevens to an offer sheet nearly twenty years prior and tried his hand at offer sheets back in 1992, attempting to bring Dave Manson over to the Washington Capitals from the Edmonton Oilers, only to see them match the offer sheet as well.

This, however, was the largest offer sheet to date in the NHL. The next closest was Thomas Vanek's seven-year, $50 million offer sheet from the Oilers that the Buffalo Sabres matched.

Poile knew that this was all a ploy to try and hang the Predators, primarily known for being frugal, out to dry.

"We're going to arrive at the same point. He's going to arrive at the same point with me," Poile said. "You're just making this an uncomfortable contract. . . I don't know why you're doing this."

According to Poile, he went straight to work, contacting Nashville's ownership group and laying out exactly what the situation was. As he knew all along and told the Flyers as much, there would be zero chance that Weber would be allowed to leave for the Flyers over an offer sheet. His contract would be matched.

He knew what the answer was going to be before he even spoke to the ownership group.

"You knew they were going to match it, right?" said Suter. "If that opportunity is out there as a player, I think you look at it. You knew that Nashville was going to sign that, so from [Weber's] standpoint I think he had that calculated. I'm sure they actually talked to him about it,

Shea Weber drops the gloves against Detroit Red Wings forward and enforcer Todd Bertuzzi.

but it's funny how everything happens and then everything changes so much and people forget about things."

On the other end of the spectrum, there was Weber. But how could you blame him for signing the offer sheet? You can't. If someone tried to lure you away from your job with a salary offer fifteen times greater than your current salary with the same benefits, hours, and amenities included, how could you say no?

"It's just one of those things in the business part of the game, I guess," said Weber. "I obviously wanted to be in Nashville. You want to stay with the team that drafts you. That's something that I think every guy wants to do, to be able to see it through.

"Things weren't developing for whatever reason and [Philadelphia] had come to the table with an offer like that. Financially it's tough to decline, but you also know you still could possibly stay in Nashville if they were to match it. Ultimately, that's what happened."

In the same respect, sometimes it's just a matter of testing the waters of free agency. Granted, Weber was one year away from having that luxury. Unlike Suter, Weber was twenty-seven at the time he signed Philadelphia's offer sheet. He was still a restricted free agent of the Nashville Predators and wasn't looking for another bridge deal that would get him one step closer to free agency.

He wanted that final contract; the one that would be the last contract he'd ever have to sign.

"The only time I ever thought I wouldn't be playing in Nashville was the uncertainty of signing the offer sheet," said Weber. "I think once the offer sheet was matched by Nashville, I honestly hoped that would be it. Every guy wants to see it through with the team that drafts you, try and win with the team that took a chance on you early in your career.

"But I don't think anyone knows what will happen, really. It's hard to stay in some situations when a guy finally becomes a free agent. It's tough not to go and see what else is out there for you."

When it came to Weber's offer sheet, it was clear it was largely about the money. Weber had made $4.5 million for the three years prior to his one-year bridge deal before the offer sheet and $7.5 million in 2011–12. He felt he was worth much more than that and opted not to file for arbitration at the July 5th deadline, one day after Suter had signed with the Wild.

Did Suter's departure play into Weber's decision to stay away from arbitration this go-around? It's fair to say that it wasn't a non-factor. Suter and Weber grew up together with the Predators. They played together in Milwaukee and forged an unyielding friendship when they were called up to Nashville. It's what made them one of the league's best defensive pairings.

To this day, Weber remains a part of Suter's life— and Suter in his, even though they no longer play on the same team and live over a thousand miles apart.

"When we play [Minnesota], I try and make a point to see him and see how things are going with him and his family," said Weber. "He's still someone I keep in touch with and try and keep up to date with how his family's doing because he was growing his family when I was with him early in Nashville. It's always nice to see them and see how they're doing."

"We talk all the time," Suter said. "We're very close and have a lot of respect for each other. It's still a very strong friendship."

The news of Suter leaving the Predators hit Weber harder than most. He had lost his defensive partner in Nashville and one of his good friends to free agency. While the Predators continued to try and make a deal happen with Weber and his agents, the hulking all-star defenseman needed some time to figure out what he was going to do next.

"He's still in disbelief," said Kevin Epp, one of Weber's agents, at the time. "They were so close this year in terms of the team's chances. They really had a shot. Shea believed there was a good chance that Ryan would stay there. So right now, Shea is still processing this news."

In the end, Weber remained with the Predators and with a young core group of players who still saw a large window of opportunity remaining to win one or multiple Stanley Cup championships in the near future.

In a press release published immediately after the news broke that Weber would be remaining with the Predators, Nashville's ownership made it clear why it was a necessity to match the offer and to match it quickly.

"The decision to enter into the largest contract in franchise history was made by all parts of the organization, including ownership, hockey operations, and business operations," the press release noted.

"We wanted to ensure that our decision reflected not just the feelings of these groups but also conveys a strong message to them that our actions would speak for us and demonstrate our commitment to them. It was absolutely essential that they understand and believe that we are doing everything possible to ice a Stanley Cup-competing team each and every season."

Philadelphia had to put out a release of their own, as well. Short and to the point, Flyers general manager Paul Holmgren released a statement.

"In tendering an offer sheet to Shea Weber, we were trying to add a top defenseman entering the prime of his career. With Nashville matching our offer, we wish Shea and the Predators all the best," Holmgren said.

Nashville had secured its future and, in doing so, proved a point across the league—one many teams hadn't seen before out of the Predators. They were going to keep their important players. It wasn't going to be similar to the fire sale in the summer of 2007; the Predators were going to do everything in their power to sign key free agents and re-sign the players that make their team successful.

In keeping Weber, they also retained one of their best locker room guys—according to any of his teammates in Nashville. Take Cody Franson for example, a childhood friend of Weber and later a teammate of his during his time with the Predators.

"The one part that I'll never forget [in Nashville] was living with Shea my first year there," said Franson. "When I first cracked the team I lived with Shea and having grown up a couple of doors down and being so close with his family, that was a pretty amazing experience for me and he kind of showed me the ropes and taught me how to be a pro. We had a lot of fun together.

"I lived with him and his wife and their two dogs and, you know, still to this day he's the guy I go to for a lot of answers when I'm going through some things and, I mean, I don't know if there's a better guy in the league to learn from, so for me to be able to have that opportunity when I was there was pretty special."

Over the course of the next four seasons, Weber would continue to drive Nashville toward its quest for a Stanley Cup championship.

After missing the playoffs in both a lockout-shortened 2012–13 season as well as the subsequent 2013–14 season—where Weber would post career-high numbers in assists and points—the Predators and Barry Trotz would part ways, bringing in Peter Laviolette and his attack-first strategy to man the helm for Nashville.

The change would serve the Predators and Weber both well, bringing Nashville back to the playoffs in just Laviolette's first season behind the bench. Although Nashville would take an early exit thanks to the Chicago Blackhawks, with Weber missing the final four games of the series, the Predators would take that confidence into a pivotal 2015–16 season—which, coincidentally, would be Weber's last with the organization.

It was his third-best season in his career, during which he notched 20 goals and 31 assists in 78 games. Heading into the playoffs, Weber and the Predators earned the top wildcard seed and faced off against the Anaheim Ducks, a team with which they had quite a familiar postseason history.

Nashville grabbed a 2–0 lead in the series before dropping three straight, having to win the next two to advance to the second round for the first time in four years.

On top of a crucial goal in game six as well as the shot that would lead to the game-winning goal in game seven, albeit deflected by teammate Paul Gaustad, the Predators would move on to face another familiar opponent in the San Jose Sharks.

Unfortunately for Weber and Nashville, it would be their final stop of the playoffs that season. With the home team winning each game, the Predators forced the series to seven games on the back of a Mike Fisher triple-overtime goal in game four and a Viktor Arvidsson overtime marker in game six. Game seven wasn't in the Predators' favor, as they were blown out 5–0 to end their season.

"They were the better team tonight," Weber said after the game. "We couldn't get anything going. It was tough. They deserved it. It was a great series back and forth, but they played better tonight."

As the year closed up for Nashville, there were zero indications that anything would be different for Weber and the blue line of the Predators—arguably the best core of defensemen in the league.

Weber headed back to his home in Kelowna, British Columbia—where he spent most offseasons playing junior hockey for the Kelowna Rockets in the four years leading up to being drafted by the Predators and then promoted to their AHL affiliate in Milwaukee.

Nearly seven weeks after exiting the playoffs against the Sharks, Weber ultimately received the biggest shock of his career: he had been traded.

"I found out through all my friends before I even talked to David Poile so there was a lot of emotions, a lot of shock certainly," said Weber.

Heading out for another gorgeous summer day in Western Canada, Weber had locked his phone in the glove box of his boat and set out for another adventure. It wasn't until many hours later that he had re-checked the glove box to see if he had missed any calls or texts that day.

His screen displayed endless notifications. Weber had missed a slew of text messages and phone calls from teammates, friends, family, and, of course, a missed call and voicemail from Poile himself.

There could have only been one situation that would have called for this.

"I had about fifty-five texts," Weber said. "James Neal was one of the guys that was at the top of the texts that I had read before, because I had a bunch of missed calls too. My phone was obviously not with me for a couple of hours and then when I got it, it was loaded with missed calls. I checked my voicemail and I had just missed a call from David [Poile] but by then it was already all over the media, so I knew what had happened at that point."

Nashville had sent Weber to the Montreal Canadiens in a one-for-one trade, with defenseman P.K. Subban returning for the Predators. It was the second time in six months that Nashville had made a player-for-player trade.

The shock would prove to be too great for Weber, as his conversation with Poile largely remains a blank spot in his memory to this day.

"To be honest with you, I don't really remember much of what David said," Weber noted. "I think I was

As of 2018, Shea Weber still holds many of Nashville's all-time franchise records—including most goals by a defenseman (166).

still in such shock. It happened so quickly and out of nowhere. There was nothing leading up to it. . . so I don't really even recall what he may have said. Everything just kind of happened so quickly, and I was trying to take it all in and digest it pretty fast."

Everyone—teammates, employees, and fans alike—thought Weber would finish his career in Nashville, exactly where it had started. No one believed that Weber, the team captain and face of the franchise for as long as he had been, would ever be traded from the organization.

As a business, though, these types of moves happen. Even when it comes to franchise players.

"I wanted to be in Nashville for my whole career," said Weber, speaking to *The Tennessean* in an interview one year after the trade. "Especially a team where you're drafted and you spend so much time, you want to bring the Stanley Cup to that city. That's your goal. . . That didn't happen."

Things aren't so bad, however. Weber's trade to the Canadiens gave the defenseman a chance to play for one of the first teams in the NHL, along with being on a team that has such a rich history.

"It's so unique. It's like the Yankees [in baseball] or the Cowboys in football," Weber said. "I think the history of this franchise and the Stanley Cups that they've won, the players, the legends that have played here, you see that every time you come in the Bell Centre. You see all the Stanley Cups they have them illuminated and mini Stanley Cups standing in front of the locker room.

"They have the wall of all their legends and players that have played here. You see them around the rink and through the concourse. It almost gives you chills when you're in there just thinking about the players that have gone through the organization and won so many titles there."

Although no longer with the Predators, Weber will forever remain a key figure in the history of the Nashville Predators. The franchise scoring records, including the 166 goals Weber scored in the 10-year span he was with the team, are prevalent in Nashville's media guide.

"We had so many good memories," Weber said when trying to determine what his favorite memory with the Predators was. "Obviously winning the first playoff series [against Anaheim], the All-Star Game in Nashville. Geez, I don't know which one to put it on. There were so many good fans and hard times as well. There's obviously a lot of blood, sweat, and tears in that city so a lot of memories that I'll never forget from playing there."

Chapter Eight

Barry Trotz's Tough Love

During the first fifteen years of Nashville's history, there was only one head coach behind the bench, one voice to command the troops for every battle they faced, every trial and every tribulation: Barry Trotz.

Let go by the Predators after the 2013–14 season and immediately hired by the Washington Capitals, Trotz left an impression on the team and community that continues to be felt to this day. More importantly, it's the way he embodied himself as a person first, coach second, that resonated more with players, media, and fans than anything else.

If you were to ask anyone around the Predators organization how they would describe Trotz using one word, you'll likely receive a plethora of differing opinions. But the general sense of the feelings will all be the same: positive, loving, caring, and personable.

He was easily one of the more respected faces in the city of Nashville while with the Predators and continues to be a respected coach in the league. For all the niceties surrounding Trotz, one thing that those who were around him most will immediately tell you is that he was straight to the point.

Sometimes it was a bit harsher than expected, but normally it was never aired to the media. Normally.

"Trotzy was never one to air his dirty laundry in public, as most coaches aren't if you're smart and you learn," said Terry Crisp, who continues to work with the Predators as a television analyst. "You don't do it. You bring them into your dressing room, but I do know this: having been a close friend of Trotzy's, I do know that he had a few one-on-ones in his dressing room, because I used to go have a coffee with him, and the paint was peeling in a lot of the corners and whatnot. So I can tell you right now, that Trotzy didn't hold the wood back when he had to, but he never went public. Only a few times that he did that."

Every player has their own little story about something that Trotz may have said to them, something that may have caught them a bit off-guard when it came out of his mouth. Many players have noted his father-like mentality when it came to the way Trotz coached, but there are always situations that, when you look back at them, make you laugh.

"I remember one time, in my first year, we flew to Columbus. It was the day before and we had burgers on the plane," said Predators defenseman Roman Josi. "I ended up eating like three burgers. I was really hungry. He gave me shit the next day for eating that many burgers. I think my body fat was a little high, too. I just think he wasn't too happy with me crushing three burgers on the flight to Columbus."

Cody Franson is one player in particular who learned the hard way that Trotz was going to be brutally honest with him, whether he liked it or not.

Defenseman Cody Franson and winger Adam Burish look on while their teammates fight.

"I have so much respect for him," Trotz said. "I was hard on him. I was absolutely, absolutely hard on him and said some things to him that were very pointed to get him to get to the next level. To this day, I've been invited to his wedding and Cody will phone me when I'm in that part of the country. In the summer, he'll touch base and to this day he'll say, 'I don't know if I would've played in the NHL if you wouldn't have did what you did and how hard you were on me to force me to get through that ceiling that I refused to go through.'"

After being drafted in 2005 by the Predators, Franson would play the next two seasons for the Vancouver Giants in the WHL before spending the better part of the next three in Milwaukee playing for Nashville's AHL affiliate, the Admirals. On his way up to playing for the Predators, though, Franson may have had one of the toughest paths, one that was largely caused by his own doing.

*   *   *   *

Trotzy's never really been like a drill sergeant-type coach, you know. Trotzy to this day is still one of the favorite people I've had as a coach. I mean, he was at my wedding. I love the guy, but, you know, that day for me was when I was trying to make the team, I had trained with Shea [Weber] all summer, you know. My year-end meeting from the year before, I had a really successful year in Milwaukee and they're like 'listen, go do the stuff that Shea does. Train with him, you know, follow him. Come back to camp and have a good camp. You've got a good chance of making the team,' so I was like ok. I'm going to do exactly what Shea did.

Shea is one of those guys that trains hard, but he's got one of those genetic builds where he doesn't need to do a ton of cardio work to be able to run circles around the track at the end of August and be totally fine. We were lifting heavy weights trying to put on size and muscle and all that kind of stuff and we were doing cardio, don't get me wrong, but less than the program called for, and then I ended up getting rear-ended in August and couldn't really do anything for a while.

I was having a good summer and I didn't want to tell Nashville because I didn't want to ruin my chance to make the team. I thought if I told them that I was in a car accident and I couldn't do anything, then they would have been like 'ah, ok, well he's not going to be ready for camp. He's going to start the year in Milwaukee,' and I didn't want to lose that chance for myself, so I didn't tell them. Long story short, I came into camp and, I was big and strong, but my body fat percentage wasn't where it needed to be, and they were very upset about it.

I didn't end up playing any exhibition games. They were sending a message. In my meeting when they went to send me down, Trotzy laid into me pretty good and questioned my heart and if I wanted it. That hit me at home. I'd never had somebody say something like that to me. Coaches say things along the way, but nobody had ever questioned that part of me and that hit home. I talked to my dad after that and I was in pretty rough shape. I went down to Milwaukee and had another good year, but they were sending their message and I didn't get any call-ups. I always respected Trotzy for it. I know that's probably not an easy thing for a coach to do, but he was never a guy to pull any punches either, which is what a lot of guys love about him.

If there was something going on, there was no bullshit with Trotzy. If you were not playing, there was a reason or if there wasn't a reason, they'd let you know. It made it easier for you to separate your home life from your work life and be able to stay in a positive mindset one way or the other.

— Cody Franson

*   *   *   *

Watching any practice or any game, you could tell the intensity that Trotz would bring. As a student of the game, he built the Predators to be a defensive-minded, heavily respected team on the ice. Sometimes, though, that intensity made its way to postgame press conferences with the media. One press conference in particular may live in infamy.

Back in his rookie season, defenseman Mattias Ekholm may have needed a bit more seasoning before a permanent stay with the Predators. After a particularly rough 5–1 Preds loss to the Vancouver Canucks early in the 2011–12 season, Ekholm drew the ire of Trotz—something that doesn't happen very often—and was directly centered in his crosshairs during a postgame scrum with the media.

"I thought he was horrible, just horrible," said Trotz, speaking to former Predators beat writer Josh Cooper of Ekholm's level of play. "You're going to have to line up against the best in the league; if you're scared of that, get a dog."

Ekholm didn't play another game for the Predators that season. Nor did he play a single game during the subsequent season. It would be nearly two full calendar years before Ekholm graced Nashville's line-up again, but after that it was to stay. After starting the season for the Predators in 2013–14, Ekholm played 62 games that year and 80 or more for the next four—including two whole seasons back-to-back without missing a game in the process.

Ultimately, Ekholm became a mainstay in Nashville's top-four on the blue line, and arguably one of the top defensemen across the league.

"You got to get stronger from it," said Ekholm. "I think you just take it as a critique as you do in everyday. I wasn't happy with my game, and there's games that I'm not happy with, so it happens every now and then. If you're a hockey player, if you can't take criticism, then you probably shouldn't be in this business. It's a part of the business, a part of the job."

At the time, Trotz's comments came off as hot-tempered, especially from a coach who was so even-keeled the majority of the time. Regardless, it may have been one of the few times that Trotz wished he could cram words back into his mouth after saying them. It was a side of Trotz that few in the media have ever seen.

"Knowing what I know of [Ekholm], I wish I would not have said that because I really like the player. I was frustrated," said Trotz. "I knew that wasn't going to hold him back; I just didn't say it the way I wanted to say it. I have remorse for the fact that it was out in public because I respect the player and his ability so much, but it was the kick in the butt that might have helped him turn the corner."

Players expected this of Trotz. He had, whether knowingly or not, set a bar with the players and staff to play the game the right way and to provide a level of honesty in both the good and the bad that he'd see on the ice. There never was mincing words with Trotz because he was clear in any type of instruction he gave to his players while in Nashville.

"Trotzy was a good player's coach. The players all respected him. He was honest," said former Predators captain Shea Weber. "He wanted you to play the right way and he expected everyone to play the right way, so I don't think there's a guy that can say to you that he wasn't honest or straightforward with something that you did or that he expected out of you.

"I think that that's not a bad thing. That's a bar that's set, a standard that's set, and I think you want all the guys to have to strive for that. I think he was really good at keeping guys accountable and keeping guys all playing for the right reasons."

There are times that Trotz would make quips during team meetings regarding the opposition. They were nothing rude or inflammatory, but comments designed to provoke a laugh from his players. More times than not, though, they closely resembled "dad jokes" than cutting-edge comedy.

As down-to-earth of a person Trotz is for those who know him, this isn't anything outside the ordinary.

"He was really good at finding ways to keep things on the team fresh," said Weber. "For a guy that's been in one place for so long, you know, guys can kind of end up tuning you out, but I think he found a way, whether it was little wisecracks like, you know, '[Jonathan] Quick is really quick.' He wasn't constantly saying the same things over and over again.

"He was willing to learn. He was willing to change philosophies, change different things to keep it fresh for the players. I think the guys really responded to that kind of stuff."

Then there is, of course, the more serious side of Trotz.

Former Predators forward Joel Ward offers one example. As training camp wound down prior to the 2008 season, Ward wasn't sure if he would be making the team with the Preds or not. Just imagine how it was when he was called in to Trotz's office.

"He called me in the office after an exhibition game," said Ward. "I didn't know what to expect, it's never a good feeling when you get called into the office, but I really didn't know. I didn't know what was happening. It was after an exhibition game and I got pulled into the office and he congratulated me and said to look for a place. I still didn't really believe it. I left the room and I remember it was pretty emotional. For my time and an emotional little period I had there, it was the first kind of glimpse that I had kind of made it. I was really excited to call my family after that to let them know about the news and kind of went on from there.

"[Trotz] was huge for me. He gave me a chance to play. Playing on a fulltime basis at that time, I really got an appreciation of who he was as a person. I thought he really cared about the individual and an easy guy to talk to if you ever have any problems or he'd be straight up with you with how you're doing. I really appreciated that, actually. It gave me a good understanding of how the league works and just kind of showed me the ropes of what it takes to play at this level."

To say he was beloved in Nashville is an understatement. Trotz still invokes plenty of great thoughts and memories from the players who played under him when he coached the Predators, to the employees of the organization, those who worked alongside his charities, and many more.

Sometimes, though, it's not necessarily a feel-good story that brings back the best memories when thinking of

Winger Joel Ward found his big break with the Predators before having successful tenures with the Washington Capitals and San Jose Sharks.

Trotz and his time with the Preds. In cases like Franson's or Ekholm's, and that of goaltender Carter Hutton, it's a swift reality check that'll do the job. The words coming from Trotz aren't the most positive, but they could easily be looked at as constructive criticism.

"I said something about Carter Hutton too, and he'll tell you that woke him up and got him to the next level," said Trotz. "I've said some things in the past that I wish

I regret, because I do feel for the person, but I have said some things and it's funny, but years later a player comes back and says 'that's what made me get over the hump. I figured it out. It kicked me in the pants. It floored me, but it made me mad and I got determined at that point.'

"I appreciate the players that years later will say 'that was the best thing for me. I hated it at the time, but it forced me to do things I didn't think I could do and I was able to do them.' I do regret some things that I say, but at the same time I'm thankful I did say them because it made the player get to where I thought they could get. Could I be more tactful? Probably? It's amazing, some of the guys that I've been the absolute hardest on in my tenure over 30 years of coaching? Those are the ones who are closer to me now because they said that was exactly what they needed and they couldn't see it when they were young."

Trotz's approach to coaching has always been that of a father figure, and he'll be the first to tell you that. For some, that type of personality when it comes from your coach can be a godsend. Others may not appreciate it as much.

His ability to take something that could potentially negatively define a player and turn it instead into a teaching moment may be one of his greatest gifts.

Take this example regarding forward Craig Smith. During the 2011 season, Smith attempted to roof a puck into an open net at the tail end of a game against the Toronto Maple Leafs—something that most players do routinely.

Instead of the puck hitting the net, it instead shot straight up and sailed into the protective netting above the glass. An easy attempt at an empty-net goal had turned horrific for a rookie only 18 games into his NHL career.

"What?" a bewildered Trotz yelled, who wasn't exactly sure what had happened. He stared toward the empty net, then up at the scoreboard, to try and catch a glimpse of exactly where the puck ended up.

"I was trying to make light of it," said Trotz. "On the bench, [Smith] was upset and I know how upset he was. I actually couldn't believe he didn't score. I gave him a minute or two and said, 'just remember what you learned there. We're not going to do that again, right?' It was a teaching moment, but obviously he wasn't in a good place after he put it up in the stands."

That type of coaching just doesn't exist anymore. It's rare to see one who connects on so many levels with the players, management, and fans that Trotz does.

"I think players absolutely understand me as a coach and probably more as a person," Trotz said. "When I say things, it's not to hurt them, but to make them better. They know I'm sort of like Dad: I'm giving them some tough love and saying some things that may be pointed, but I think they do believe that I love them and it's about them, not me.

"It's never about me, it's about them. How they can be better and how I want them to be better. It's my job to make them better in any way I can. If it's being hard, I'll be hard. If it's giving them an arm around the shoulder and teaching and talking, I'll do that. But I think they believe that I have their best interest in my mind. I could care less about a lot of things that a lot of coaches may care about. I care about the person first."

Chapter Nine

Tragedy in Chicago

Hockey is a game of inches. If anyone were to tell you differently, have them sit down and watch any second of hockey during the Stanley Cup playoffs. In the playoffs, better teams can lose and the unexpected is always bound to happen.

Nashville's young, but budding, history already has key moments that have shaped this franchise—both for the better and for the worse.

If you were to ask any long-time Predators fan about Game Five during the 2010 postseason, their face would surely drop and a largely painful story would be recounted about the missed opportunity for Nashville and one that would define the playoffs for the Chicago Blackhawks.

The 2009–10 season was one of streaks for the Preds. It was also the same year that goaltender Pekka Rinne would solidify himself as Nashville's starting net-minder for years to come.

After starting the season winning back-to-back games, then losing seven of the next eight, Nashville would rattle off winning streaks of seven, six, and then multiple streaks of four and three, while equally losing in streaks of three and five. A tough January would put the Predators just a handful of games over .500, before Nashville would finish the season over the last two months losing back-to-back games only twice in that span.

Facing the Blackhawks in the first round of the play-offs wasn't a foregone conclusion, either. The Predators had won three of their final four games—two against the St. Louis Blues and one over the Detroit Red Wings who were just ahead of them in the standings. All Nashville needed was a regulation or overtime loss for the Los Angeles Kings to the Colorado Avalanche and the Preds would start their postseason heading to Vancouver against the Canucks.

With a better seeding on the line for the Kings, Los Angeles would watch as Dustin Brown put a shot past then-Avalanche goaltender Craig Anderson for a 2–1 victory in overtime, sealing the six seed for the Kings and handing the Predators a trip to Chicago where they would face the Central Division champion Blackhawks.

Of the four previous trips to the playoffs for the Predators, they had yet to record a road victory. They hadn't won more than two games in a series, never had a series lead, and, more importantly, never advanced past the first round.

For a team that most had picked to be handily sacked by the Blackhawks, the visitors started it out with a bang—leaving fans in the United Center wondering what just happened.

Nashville grabbed a 1–0 series lead over the Blackhawks after a two-goal performance from J.P. Dumont and two empty-netters sealed the deal.

The teams would alternate wins and losses through the next three games, setting up a pivotal Game Five in

Colin Wilson, who played with the Predators from 2009 until 2017, races around Blackhawks defenseman Brent Seabrook.

the Windy City, where the winner would swing the series in their favor.

Most of the players involved can still remember nearly every detail about this game, with only a cursory reference to the date April 24, 2010.

"Is that the one where [Marian] Hossa hit [Dan] Hamhuis from behind?" said defenseman Cody Franson. "Yeah, I had a front-row seat to that one."

It wasn't just a normal game for Nashville. This was a game where the players felt they could come out with a win and sew the series up at home against Chicago—one where they could give the fans back in Nashville something they had yet to see in the seemingly short history of the franchise.

The night started off as well as it could for the Predators—seeing David Legwand collect the first goal of the night 6:23 into the first period, putting the Blackhawks on notice. Five minutes later, Chicago would turn things around.

With the Hawks consistently pressuring in the offensive zone, Blackhawks defenseman Brent Seabrook rifled a shot towards the net. After the puck deflected and bounced away from Rinne, Andrew Ladd swiped it back into the yawning net, tying the game at one.

Minutes after that, defenseman Niklas Hjalmarsson blasted one from the point past Rinne for a 2–1 Chicago lead—one that would remain intact for the rest of the first period.

Things wouldn't get much better for the Predators from there. The shot counter would reflect as much.

With a too-many-men penalty expiring on Chicago, Tomas Kopecky exited the box right as the puck had been cleared down the ice by Marian Hossa. Ryan Suter was victimized on the play, not having noticed a racing Kopecky streamlining to the cleared puck. A failed poke-check by Rinne, followed by a deke by Kopecky would give the Blackhawks a 3–1 lead—something that tends to be insurmountable for most visiting teams at the United Center.

Nashville wasn't ready to throw in the towel.

Just over a minute after the third Blackhawks goal, Legwand and Joel Ward converted on a shorthanded two-on-one opportunity to make it a one-goal deficit heading into the third period.

Ninety-four seconds into the third, Nashville defenseman Denis Grebeshkov found Dumont off to the left side of the net, where he slid the puck to forward Martin Erat in the slot, finishing off a tic-tac-toe play to tie the game at three. Ten minutes later, Grebeshkov again set up another third-period goal, dishing the puck to Erat off the left side of goaltender Antii Niemi and finishing the play—giving Nashville a 4–3 lead with 8:21 left in regulation.

All the Predators needed to do from here was hold off a potential Blackhawks onslaught toward Rinne and collect the win. They knew Chicago was going to put every last remaining ounce of energy on the table to end this game. Both teams knew what was at stake.

Locking into a defensive approach for the final eight minutes, the Predators were content to drive the Blackhawks out and force pucks through the neutral zone to set up chances at running the clock off while trying to tally one more goal to stretch the lead.

In the final minutes of regulation, Chicago made a critical error: Marian Hossa, one of the more dangerous Blackhawks forwards on the ice, would head to the box for boarding Dan Hamhuis with 63 seconds to go—a five-minute major leaving the Blackhawks shorthanded. Even if they were able to somehow miraculously tie the game in the final minute, they'd still be shorthanded for the first four minutes of overtime.

The Predators could sense it. The game was going to shift in their favor with a chance to end the series on home ice.

"I know when Hossa took that penalty, I think everyone on the bench was saying holy crap, now we're going to have to win game six and seven to move on out of the first round," said former Blackhawks forward Kris Versteeg. "I didn't really know how it was going to work.

I think sometimes you expect guys to be ejected and generally it's the ref's discretion. I didn't really know what was going on. When it happened, we thought the game's probably over."

Get the puck into the offensive zone and keep it there—that was the message. Nashville's power play had yet to score a goal the entire series, but all it needed to do was prevent anything disastrous from happening and a good pat on the back and "job well done" would be levied to the players on the ice.

But hockey is a game of inches. And in the playoffs? Anything can happen, and most certainly does.

Blackhawks captain Jonathan Toews won the initial faceoff in the defensive zone after the Hossa major, but Seabrook lost the puck to the Predators just seconds later.

Fifty-seven seconds to go.

After cycling the puck around, Shea Weber dumped the puck cross-ice and deeper into the Blackhawks zone.

Forty seconds to go.

Jason Arnott, then captain for the Predators, raced over to grab the loose puck, passing it back to Suter at the blue line. Suter, like his partner moments ago, fired it cross-ice deep towards the opposite corner.

Thirty-five seconds to go. The seconds seemed like minutes, an eternity for Nashville to seal the deal with a win and finally head back home.

Ward and Blackhawks defenseman Duncan Keith sped toward the corner to battle for the puck, seeing Keith get there a fraction of a second too late while Ward hip-checked him to slightly poke the puck toward an incoming Erat, who had room to work with behind the goal.

Thirty-three seconds to go. As innocuous as it seemed, a simple pass right at this moment would doom the Predators in the swing game of the series and the series itself. But to this day, what happened next remains a haunting sequence of events for Predators players who were there.

As Erat skated in to grab the puck from Ward, he checked to see exactly which players on the ice were available to pass it off to behind him. Noticing that Arnott was cutting across the slot toward his general vicinity, and with Seabrook closing in quickly from the opposite side of the net, Erat attempted to drop a pass back to Arnott. It would have left the Predators captain wide open in front of an unsuspecting Niemi, offering a chance to bury a major powerplay marker and give Nashville a 5–3 lead.

Something was off, though. The angle of the pass was sharper than Erat had intended.

Instead of feeding it back and finding Arnott in the slot, Erat's pass banked off the side of the net and bounced right to the stick of Toews, who quickly turned and exited the zone.

Thirty seconds to go.

"The end of the game, as much as we didn't want to admit it, was a little bit of panic," recalled Dumont, who continues to live in Nashville and coaches youth hockey now. "We can be up 3–2 on Chicago. It was crazy. We knew that someone was going to try to leave the zone, but we were still playing reckless and it was not the greatest play."

Patrick Kane, who had been held to a single assist the entire night, left the other Hawks on the ice to fend for the defensive zone while he skated through center ice waiting for an unlikely shorthanded breakout play.

With Toews streamlining towards the opposite end of the ice, drawing the focus of both Weber and Suter, Kane circled through Nashville's end—watching Niemi head off the ice for an extra attacker.

Twenty-seven seconds to go.

Toews gained the zone under the watchful eye of Weber, followed closely behind by Arnott. Circling back around after Weber cut off his path prior to the face-off circle to Rinne's right, Toews found Seabrook entering the zone and sent a pass his way—putting it toward the net.

Deflected by Keith, the shot ramped up, bounced off the crossbar behind Rinne, hit the boards, and fell to the ice.

Twenty seconds to go.

Rushing behind the net, Erat scooped the puck up and fired it across the boards, attempting to clear it out of the zone. Patrick Sharp, the Blackhawks extra attacker, barely got enough of the puck to slow its pace, giving him a chance to corral it back into the play.

Eighteen seconds to go.

With the play unfolding 30 feet away from the net, Ward had a clear line-of-sight on Kane—who had planted himself directly to Rinne's right, waiting for any type of rebounds from shots toward the net. He skated over in position to cover Kane, checking behind him to make sure he was in the right area.

Fifteen seconds to go.

Sharp chipped the puck to Seabrook, who passed it to Toews, firing at the net as soon as the puck hit the blade of his stick.

"Shot by Toews, rebound, score! Kane!" yelled an emphatic Doc Emerick, NBC's longtime NHL play-by-play announcer, as the goal horn blew inside the United Center.

13.6 seconds to go.

Nashville was exhausted. The fatigue and disgust was visible on the players' faces as the Hawks celebrated and the Predators were left to wonder what the hell just happened when they were cycling the puck in the Chicago zone just 20 seconds prior.

The horn sounded, regulation ended, and both teams headed back to their locker rooms with a chance to settle the game in overtime. Nashville would have nearly four minutes of power play time to start the extra period.

"Those are things you better learn and you better realize that hey, sixty minutes, not fifty-nine and a half, sixty minutes is what it takes to take home the Cup, every night," said former Predators color analyst Terry Crisp, who called the game alongside play-by-play broadcaster Pete Weber.

"It was disappointing. We worked so hard and knew we had them. We had them down and out. Again, what we didn't learn was that they're never down and out. Like Detroit never used to be when they had the guns. At that given time they had Kane and Toews and Sharp and a few of those guys that could hurt you in the dying minutes of a hockey game, or seconds."

Even with the opportunity to finish the game on a positive note during the overtime period, Kane's goal seemingly sucked all the momentum away from the Predators and put it solely on the Blackhawks. There was a calming sense inside the locker room, however, as if the Preds were just a fortunate bounce away from taking this game—regardless of what had just happened.

"We were fortunate in a sense that we had some older guys in our room that kept that situation relatively calm," said Franson. "To get scored on in that situation, I felt we went into overtime and the guys weren't panicking. We wanted to win it in regulation, you know. You're on your heels a little bit going into that because you can't believe what just happened, but I thought we handled it pretty well."

As the puck dropped for the first overtime, Nashville did everything it could to focus on peppering Niemi with as much puck traffic as possible.

Get into the zone, set the play up, fire a puck on net. Traffic, traffic, traffic, traffic.

It just didn't work out that way.

Outside of a few decent chances on Niemi, the Predators couldn't keep the puck in the offensive zone, watching the seconds tick away on their man-advantage. With Hossa's power play expiring, the Hawks trapped Nashville in their own zone and began cycling the puck around looking for a way to end the game.

Hossa skated right behind Rinne, almost in the same position Kane was in for the game-tying goal, and waited for the play to assemble. With Chicago forward Dave Bolland circulating the puck around behind the net, he passed the puck off to the point where defenseman Brent Sopel waited patiently to get a shot off.

Sopel's shot careened off the stick of Ward, deflected straight to Hossa—instead of where Rinne had thought the puck was going—and was easily popped to the back of the net.

Game. 5–4 Blackhawks. Chicago led the series three games to two.

"We had the power play and I thought we were just kind of moving around trying to kill time," said then-Predators defenseman Shea Weber. "They made a good play getting a stick on the puck when it went in through the box there. They got the goalie pulled, they're in the zone for what didn't seem like very long and then they scored to tie it up and eventually won in overtime. Those are the momentum shifts in playoff games that really, ultimately win you series and eventually Stanley Cups."

Whatever hope Nashville had of finishing strongly, or even getting a playoff series win, seemed to evaporate in a span of five minutes.

"We just couldn't find a way. I really believe that goal popped our balloon; it was a killer goal that killed every hope we had," said Dumont.

"That was extremely disappointing. It was like it took all the air out and kind of deflated the whole team, and after that the series was done right then, but it was a good learning experience too," Rinne said. "For that entire summer it stayed in my mind. It was extremely disappointing."

Two days later, Nashville's fears of game five haunting them came to fruition. A back-and-forth first period would see both teams exchange goals, including a fluky dump pass from Seabrook that banked off the skate of Kane and easily slid past a confused Rinne, ending with a power play goal from Toews to give Chicago a 4–3 lead after 20 minutes.

"We win [game five] and we're coming back home with the series lead. It could be a completely different result," said Weber. "Those are reasons why good teams find ways to win, and I think it was a learning lesson for a lot of guys because it was tough for us to bounce back."

"The life was just sucked right out of us in game five. That was probably one of the most devastating losses for a lot of guys on our team knowing what we could have had, but at the end of the day we still may have been able to come back and win in seven if we had won that game. Nothing's guaranteed, but I think we were mentally pretty hard on ourselves and the next thing you know an unfortunate bounce ends up in your net and it just seems like it's just piling up and things just aren't going to go your way."

That lead would hold until the Blackhawks notched an empty-net goal in the final seconds of the third period.

"I thought going into the series we took them too lightly. We knew they were a good team and we were young and maybe a little too cocky going into that series and they kind of put us in our place," said Versteeg. "We used a few lucky bounces and moments to come out of that series and I think that was our toughest series I'd say, for sure. I think in the four [rounds], personally. I think some guys might have different views, but I thought it was the only series I think that could have been in limbo."

There's no telling what would have happened had Nashville won that Game Five or even pushed the series to seven games had they held off the Hawks on home ice. What they did learn, however, was to never quit until the final horn sounds. And for some like general manager David Poile, it's a moment that sits high in terms of heartbreak.

"That's right near the top. Right near the top," Poile said. "That was a situation that was hard to recover from. Very hard to recover from. Should've been a win with the power play and our players did not manage that situation well at that time."

Nashville had another hard-fought series with the Blackhawks in 2015, again being ousted in six games. Chicago again went on to win the Stanley Cup.

"We came out on the wrong side of it," said Franson, on losing to Chicago during the 2015 season. "Being a young guy in that situation, though, you do notice the older guys taking charge in the room when the stakes are so high like that. I mean, going into that, that's when Chicago was at their peak and we knew that if we could beat Chicago we'd give ourselves a chance.

"I think if you were to ask guys on the Chicago side of that series, I think they'd probably tell you that our series was probably the hardest one that they played on that run. Unfortunate the way it worked out, but it is what it is."

It was a lesson the team took with them in the years to come, including the very next season where Nashville would win its first playoff series in franchise history. Are these moments ingrained in players' minds? Are they ones that they'll remember throughout their playing career?

"You know what, I don't know if it ingrains on them," said Crisp. "It sure makes you open your eyes and say you know what? If we had stayed or got the puck out of our zone or if we had made the right play around the boards, that's what I always remember as a player. What did I do? What we should have done. What could have happened to make it through it? But the biggest thing is I always say to remember it, but don't dwell on it. We know what we have to do now and let's do it."

There were a handful of situations that, had they gone differently, the Predators would have been the ones to have advanced in 2010 and Chicago winning a Stanley Cup that year wouldn't have happened. But they didn't. And what if Hossa were to have been ejected for that hit instead of serving the five-minute major and coming back out to score the game-winning goal?

Just another example of hindsight. In the end, though, it's just the way it was to be written.

"I know our coaches and everybody was pretty fired up that [Hossa] never got kicked out," said Franson. "To have him come out of the box and score like that was pretty aggravating. But you know what? That's history. What can you do?"

Chapter Ten

The Greatest Stories of Gnash

One of the most iconic faces of the franchise is actually that of the team's mascot. Clad in his own Nashville Predators jersey with "00" stitched on the back, Gnash, a blue-skinned sabretooth tiger modeled after the remains of a sabre-toothed cat found nearly forty years ago during construction in downtown Nashville, can be seen swinging from the rafters and high-fiving fans throughout each Predators game.

As the seasons progress, Gnash has been one of the few mainstays within the organization. There's never been another mascot for the team. They've never needed to have another.

Gnash himself would be the first to tell you that he leads an interesting life. From the on-the-ice antics to the off-the-ice visits and trips that he makes, there isn't much that Gnash hasn't done in the twenty years the Nashville Predators have been around.

Prior to the arrival of both the Predators and the Tennessee Titans of the NFL, there was a major lack of any true draw for entertainment purposes in Nashville. You could constitute that the Grand Ole Opry and Opryland, a since-defunct amusement park on the outskirts of the city itself, were heavy draws for tourism, but since the arrival of Nashville's two professional sports teams, the need for entertainment in the city has most definitely been filled.

"The team does such an amazing job of fulfilling the city's need for entertainment," said Gnash. "Nashville is an entertainment city, and win, lose, or draw, you have to entertain the fans, and they have done such a phenomenal job with that. There is so much energy and excitement that we would have to work really hard to have a bad event."

Planning Gnash's every move has become more meticulous over the years as the mascot has risen in popularity. There are mainstay skits that fans have grown accustomed to seeing—climbing the ladder to the tune of the Cliffhangers game from *The Price is Right*, the "Evolution of Dance," and the always classic pie in the face to a visiting fan. There are also plenty of new skits that have come along over the course of the past couple of seasons.

Gnash says that most skit ideas that he comes up with are rarely rejected.

"The only ideas that they passed on were because they were too long," Gnash said. "We ended up doing an intermission Christmas show where we had flying reindeer and a sleigh that came down out of the ceiling, all this aerial stuntwork, and I always wanted to pitch bigger, grander ideas and I typically got shot down because, 'Hey, Gnash, we've got a ninety-second timeout you got to fill, we can't bring in a marching band in ninety seconds.'"

In one particular case, Gnash details how he caught some of his colleagues by surprise with one of his ideas:

I did an Australian Rappel, which is instead of having the carabiner and the connection in front right at your waist, you put the connection on your waist at your back, so you're flat like Superman. I didn't tell anyone that I was doing an Australian Rappel. You've seen the videos. I'd come down fast, upside down, head first, and then, you know, slow down at the bottom and flip over and stand on the ice.

With the Australian Rappel, it looks like someone falling because you're in that classic freefall pose. I didn't tell anyone. I jumped and intentionally flailed my arms and legs like I had fallen. As I got closer to the ice than I ever had, maybe six or eight feet before I started to break, I stopped inches off the ice. I was so close I couldn't even stand up. I had to put my hands down on the ice and then come down to my knees and stand up, but because I was going so fast and stopped so much further, when I pulled the rope across my body to stop, I burned through my jersey.

That was one where I thought you know, that was, that was a little too much. I don't need to do that again. I do a stunt, everybody's ready, and there's the PA. Usually I hear "Yaaaay!" from the crowd. This was "Yaa-AAAAAAH!!", a pause, and you could hear the gasp in the arena. Of course, when I didn't die, everybody roared.

During a normal game night. While the puck is stopped, Paul McCann, Nashville Predators public address announcer, or Maverick, the in-arena host, will draw the attention of the crowd to wherever Gnash is at the given moment.

Gnash describes one particularly memorable occurrence:

> There was a little boy in the upper deck. I don't remember his name, but he was born without hands, and of course everybody high-fives. I go through and high-five everybody. You know, fist bumps weren't a thing back then, and I just distinctly remember this little boy so wanted to connect but with his birth defect, you know, clearly was different, shy, and reserved.
>
> I'm not claiming to have created the fist-bump, but in that moment, that was the connection with him, and he and I had a fist-bump. After that, he would find me before every game. His parents ultimately became season ticket holders because their son wanted to go to every game and I would visit him in the upper deck and . . . if he wasn't there, you know, the entire section up in the upper deck would find me and they'd say 'Oh, he's not here today. He's not here' or 'Hold on, he's in the bathroom. Don't leave yet.' Having those kinds of connections are the ones that make it all worth it.

Most may not realize that Gnash is multi-talented in terms of how he's able to communicate with fans of all different backgrounds. Although largely mute and utilizing the help of his handlers to speak with fans that come up with requests during games, Gnash finds a way to make all fans feel like they're a part of his family.

It's that particular demonstration of inclusivity that largely leads Gnash to be one of the more popular figures in the city of Nashville, mascot or not.

Predators mascot Gnash has been the only mascot in team history. He's routinely been labeled as one of the best mascots across the league.

He explains:

The Preds used to have a Deaf Awareness Night and the deaf community would come out and there would be group seats and there would be different elements where there was sign language or signage or something. . .

Whether it was a Deaf Awareness Night or not, I always made it a point to go into the sections where that community was and share that and let them know that I knew sign language and just to make a connection with the community.

I got a letter after one of the games and what had happened was I went into the section and there happened to be a family there: mom and dad, a younger brother—elementary school age—and a high school age daughter. I came into the section and immediately recognized that Mom and Dad were deaf, the son and daughter were not . . .

The parents were so amazed that I was signing that all of my focus was on them. We were interacting together. We were having a conversation, which no one else can do because I don't speak, but I could have an actual conversation through sign language with Mom and Dad and have jokes and fun.

I got a letter a few days later that they had been having a lot of problems with their daughter because she was not part of the deaf community. She could hear. A lot of it, I'm sure, was just traditional teenage angst but it was really impacting their family pretty heavily. There had been just an absolute one-eighty after that game because I knew sign language. I was there for her parents. I was someone she associated with something cool and something impressive and big and professional. I was part of the deaf community, and I was connecting not with her and her friends, but with her parents and that there was a newfound respect and connection with her parents.

✱   ✱   ✱   ✱

There's also Gnash's role in visiting the sick that has become of great importance in the Nashville community. For anyone with a role as an entertainment figure, paying visits to fans who are ailing or even terminally ill often becomes a necessity. These fans, a large contingent of whom are children, hope that these sports figures can lift their spirits, even if it's just for a short moment.

Predators, in addition to Gnash, visit the Monroe Carell Jr. Children's Hospital at Vanderbilt often multiple times a season to cater to the multitude of children who are there, as well as their parents and families. The connection that is made during the visits, especially in Gnash's case, is the reason these are so important.

As he recalls,

The hospital visits were always the tough, happy moments because sometimes you know you're in a terminal ward, but you're there to give them smiles and you make them happy. The tough moments come days and weeks later.

There was a little girl in the hospital that I went to see, and just, she smiled, it was wonderful, there were hugs, and she actually came out of her room, chased me down a hallway with her IV tree, and wanted one more hug before the ele-

vator. I got a letter a week later that that was the
last smile that she had and that was the last time
her family had all been there.

The family was writing me a letter to thank
me for that being the last memory they had. By
the end of that day, she was gone. But their image
of her, the image that was burned into their head,
was that smile and that laughter, and I'd given
that to them.

Such a memory is sobering to consider. Yet, after
nearly twenty years of these hospital visits, Gnash continues to go and put smiles on these faces.

*   *   *   *

For all of the positive memories and the impact that
Gnash has had on the community, there are always
the opposing fans who don't react the same way to the
home mascot.

As Gnash explains,

We played Chicago years ago and that was back
when they used to bus people in. People would
come in and you'd have a whole section [of
visiting fans]. We don't really do that now. We
don't have the inventory and we kind of learned
our lesson: you don't let people buy a whole
section of tickets.

Some Chicago fans were pretty drunk and
we went up there to visit somebody and they

kind of came over starting trouble. I kind of mocked them, turned around, one Chicago fan pushed me from behind, and then I mocked him some more. I turned around and then there was a group of Preds fans behind him. It's almost like two sections were diverging at each other and it was almost like a *West Side Story* type, you know [snaps fingers], we're getting ready to rumble type thing.

I had an assistant who played football at Nebraska, so I thought this big guy has got my back. He's nowhere to be found. He's down on the radio panicking calling for security trying to get security up there, but ushers came up there and cooler heads prevailed and it was shut down, but it was pretty scary. It was third period and people were drunk. Alcohol does crazy things to people.

Most of the time, those opposing fans just want a picture. They just want a picture and that's changed the job more than anything. You used to walk around the arena and you could go from section to section and nobody would bother you. People would high-five you, you could entertain, you could do whatever. Now, everybody wants a picture. Everybody wants a snap or something for Instagram. It's a social media-driven world and there's no better way to say "I was at a game" than to get a picture with a mascot.

Yet hockey fans aren't the only ones that want to get in on the ambiance surrounding Gnash—sometimes hockey players want to be a part of it as well.

And sometimes, the hockey player in question may, in fact, be arguably the greatest player to ever play the game.

According to Gnash:

> One of my coolest moments was beating Wayne Gretzky at bubble hockey. Yeah, bubble hockey's my game. . .
>
> They had contests where you got to play bubble hockey tournaments and you got to meet Wayne Gretzky if you won. Well we got there early and we were waiting on a Preds fan to come that got to play and meet Wayne Gretzky and we were warming up bubble hockey. So he wanted to play and I just smoked him. Smoked him at bubble hockey. So that's Gnash's claim to fame is that he beat Wayne Gretzky at hockey.
>
> Then Wayne, at that game, requested Gnash for a picture, wanted Gnash to come to his suite for a picture so Gnash is a celebrity. I, of course, went up there to get a picture with Wayne and his wife, and of course he told his wife how Gnash killed him at bubble hockey and everything.

Gnash attends over 900 appearances each year. There are the visits to the hospital and the birthday parties for kids. Those are routine. But then you have the wedding invitations, which come from across the country—many from Tennessee, some from Florida, North Carolina, Wisconsin, and across the United States. He's an incredibly popular mascot off the ice.

What never gets old, though, are the prom appearances. And, better yet, the times where Gnash acts as a prom date. As he explains:

I've been a prom date two or three times. I went to Harpeth Hall and then they do this little thing where they, you go to this gym and they have this little runway and they say, introduce the girl, and then they introduce, 'escorted by' whoever her date is. It's mainly for the parents. You get to this part where they come on the stage and they say, you know, 'Cindy Lou Who escorted by Tommy' and then they get to the girl and it was like 'Jamie so-and-so escorted by Gnash' and the place went nuts.

They put the spotlight in her face and obviously when the spotlight's right in your face you can't see anything so of course I tripped going up the stairs, which everybody thinks is part of the gag and laugh, and then you escort her out, walk her back, and then of course Gnash takes his own turn around the catwalk doing his little thing and she had a ball. She had a ball and you're there for about an hour. You take pictures, lots of pictures, lots and lots of pictures, and then dance a little bit and then you're done.

It's tough to imagine what this franchise would be like without the existence of Gnash and what he's done for not only the team, but for Nashville and the hockey community as a whole.

That's the life of a hockey mascot, though. Some, like Montreal's Youppi! and Anaheim's Wild Wing, are legendary for what they do both on and off the ice. Sometimes it just takes a bit of a personal touch to really go the extra mile.

Luckily, for the Predators and their fanbase, Gnash gets it. He always has.

Chapter Eleven

Hockey Nicknames Are Fun

Hockey nicknames are a big deal. From all the nuances surrounding an 82-game season—pre-game rituals, choices of restaurants, music playlists, how one tapes his stick, and more—none may be more important than how a player earns a nickname.

Most may not know that players often have multiple nicknames over the course of each season. Generally, it's a way to keep things fresh in the locker room and to break the monotony.

The genesis behind nicknames range from tame to not-meant-for-print. Yet some stand above the rest.

For example, right wing Austin Watson provided the nickname of "Randy" to left wing Kevin Fiala during the 2017–18 season.

"[Watson] called me Randy," said Fiala. "It's because last year I kind of had a hat with the word 'Savage' on it."

Randy Savage, whose real name is Randall Poffo, was a professional wrestler better known by his ring name of "Macho Man" for both the World Wrestling Entertainment and World Championship Wrestling. To Fiala, though, he initially had no clue who Savage was or why he was named Randy. It seemed like just an odd nickname at the time.

"I didn't know what it meant before [it was explained]," Fiala said. "Now, though, I know."

During his tenure with the Predators, Shea Weber was quite the author of many nicknames for his teammates, most that never saw the light of day. Given Weber's quiet demeanor off the ice, he wouldn't necessarily be the first person you'd expect to make up new names for his teammates.

"I think [Weber] would just say whatever came to him," said defenseman Ryan Suter.

That was Weber not only trying to interject his own brand of humor into the locker room, but also trying to be the captain and leader of the team.

"I think I tend to call people a lot of things," said Weber. "It's kind of just whatever comes out. You don't really think too hard about it. It's just kind of something that seems to come to mind and sticks and fits and, I don't know. It's kind of funny. Guys relate to it. It could be so ridiculous it doesn't make any sense but it's funny and it sticks. Some of them don't work too, you know, like it kind of doesn't fit and it doesn't really go anywhere."

In addition to nicknames, players try to find other activities that motivate them during the latter portion of the season.

"There's a number of different things that you do," Weber noted. "Guys get into February or March where it just kind of seems like Groundhog Day sometimes.

Sometimes it gets kind of gray [in Nashville] for a bit and the weather's not great. You have to try to find things for guys to do. Whether that was where we've gone bowling as a team or go-karts, different things kind of keep it fresh and things that kind of liven things up when things are kind of getting stale throughout the year."

Former Nashville defenseman Cody Franson became the target of a Shea Weber nickname while playing for the Predators. It was Weber's way of poking fun at a story that Franson had told him, yet it also became a source of humor for the rest of the team as the story made its way through the locker room.

"Weber always called me 'Humes', which is short for 'Human,'" said Franson, laughing as he recalled how the name was given to him. "We were in dinner in St. Louis and Webs always thought this was kind of funny. When I moved out of the house when I was 15 to go play hockey, my mom was really sad. So my dad bought a dog for the family after I moved out and let my mom name it. She ended up naming the dog Franny."

Franny remains the main nickname for Franson to this day. Like most players, they'll often be called a mixture of their last name, trimmed to add one to two conso-nants at the end, mostly an s: Webs for Weber, Sutes for Suter, Franny for Franson. Those are just a few examples.

"So Webs thought that was hilarious and he kind of kept it to himself for a while," Franson continued. "Then all of a sudden one day we were having lunch in St. Louis, having a pregame meal, and he goes 'Hey, Kleiner [defenseman Kevin Klein]. Guess what Franny's family's dog's name is?'"

"Kleiner's like 'What?' And I'm like 'Webs, you motherfucker.' And he goes 'Franny.' So I was asked what my dog's name was again. I was like, 'it's Franny.' Klein goes, 'wait, so there's a Franny dog and a Franny human?" I'm like "Yep." And that's where 'Human' came from and then 'Humes' for short."

Whether he wanted that nickname out there or not, it was there to stay, courtesy of a guy he had known since childhood.

"I kind of just kept to myself and accepted it and tried to make it what it was," said Franson.

Some players, like forward Ryan Johansen, happen to have a number of names at any given point in a season, but not all of them are out in the open

"Some nicknames we can say publicly. The public ones are Joey, which I've had since the start," Johansen said during the 2017–18 season. "Some guys call me Joe. My middle name's Baltimore so some people think it's funny to call me Baltimore, which it's not. It hurts my feelings."

I could tell that last part was him just being the naturally funny guy that he is, as some of the players changing in the locker room around him started to tune into our conversation.

"Johandsome. Most people call me Johandsome," Johansen proclaimed.

When the validity of the nickname was questioned, however, a teammate found the opportunity to interject.

"Johandsome?" questioned forward Scott Hartnell. "I've never heard that before in my life and I've been with you for three years."

During the discussion that ensued, Johansen, Hartnell, and a handful of other players went back and forth on the subject for what seemed like a handful of minutes, most attempting to dispute Johansen's claims while Johansen himself maintained his argument that it was an oft-used nickname.

"That's kind of a thing," said Johansen. "When you're with each other every day all year long, you come in mornings and you just start saying stuff because you see them every day and you don't even know what to say to them anymore. There's a lot of weird comments we get in our dressing room which is what makes it so funny.

"I had a Martin's BBQ hat on the other day from where we had our team party at the start of the year, and everybody that day just decided to call me Marty. That's just kind of how it goes around here."

"You always got to be watching your back," Johansen joked.

Sometimes, players may have no clue how they acquired a new name in the locker room.

"Guys in here call me Walter, but I don't know why," said forward Austin Watson.

"I don't really know exactly why. I can be a little grumpy in the mornings. I'm not a morning person, so I don't know if it has to do with something like that. I get the Muppets, Walter the Muppet. Some guys think it's because of that. I'm not exactly sure."

Something that's evident is that once you're a player, or even a coach, you have a bit of carte blanche to continue with nicknames after your career is over—even if you continue to work with an organization after your playing days are over.

Terry Crisp is a prime example of this. Crispy, as he's so eloquently referred to around the Predators organization, has been with Nashville since the inaugural season. If a player has thrown on a jersey for the Preds, odds are Crisp has analyzed his play at one point and likely added his own personal nickname to some of them.

"Scotty Hartnell was one of my first favorites," said Crisp. "When he first came here, eighteen years old, Pete [Weber] and I dubbed him 'Baby Bull' and he was a baby bull out there. He hit everything that moved, and if it didn't move he hit it until it did.

"The other guy we liked was Vladimir Orszagh. We called him The Little Slovakian Tank. He was like [Viktor] Arvidsson, a precursor of Arvidsson and [Miikka] Salomaki all rolled into one. We loved him."

Crisp would often relay these names when talking to these players off the ice after games or practices, as his rapport with those in and around the locker room is largely indescribable.

After Hartnell was brought back to the Predators with a new contract prior to the 2017–18 season, a gap of nearly 10 seasons away from the club, did Crisp still call him "baby bull"?

"Now I call him Grandpa Bull," laughed Crisp.

Every player and coach has his or her own story behind each nickname given to them. Most of these nicknames are innocuous in nature. There's "Sutes" and "Webs." "Jos" and "Subby." "Leggy," "Nealer," "Watty," and, yes, even "Horny."

Let's face it—sometimes jobs can become boring. Sometimes you just need to have a little fun to lighten the mood.

Chapter Twelve

Standing Ovations: Nashville's Hockey Pastime

As the Predators headed into the final months of the 2006–07 season, Nashville found itself fighting to stay atop the Central Division alongside the powerhouse Red Wings—winners of six of the previous seven division titles. With his team floundering to stay afloat in February, general manager David Poile wanted to make a splash to show ownership and fans that the Preds would be buyers that season.

Always hotly-contested amidst some of Nashville's more die-hard fans, the trade for legendary forward Peter Forsberg arguably stands as the first true power trade in Poile's tenure as Predators general manager and one the fans hoped would boost the team into the upper echelon of the league.

"That might have been the second most exciting time in our franchise history," laughed Poile. "It just was one of those situations where he just had that rock star quality with our players, with our fans, with the media. He had that swagger and he was Peter Forsberg and it was a dynamic time even though he was at the tail end of his career.

"We had Paul Kariya on the same team and they're both hall of famers as it turns out. That was a huge plus for our franchise. It was a time when everything was just ok. It was a huge commitment what we gave up to get Peter, but also I think it kind of put us on the map with our fans and, you know, it wasn't one of those 'are we going in the right direction?' things."

Nashville wouldn't earn its first Central Division title that season, nor any time in the next decade, and the splash for one of the best forwards to play the game didn't pay off as the Predators were bounced that season by the San Jose Sharks in five games. It marked the second season in a row the Sharks knocked Nashville out in the first round, both times only taking five games.

What happened next nobody could have scripted.

The Predators were on the cusp of something no one who worked for or had supported the organization for the past decade could have dreamed of: packing up the franchise and moving.

Unlike the current age of the franchise, where Nashville has reaped the fruits of its labor —triple-digit sellout streaks, season ticket waiting lists, one of the hottest venues in North America—there was a time after the 2004–05 lockout where the organization only found itself selling out the building when one of the Original Six teams came to play, most of those coming via the Red Wings as their divisional opponent.

After falling to the Sharks in the 2007 playoffs, the Preds found that all the off-the-ice misfortunes surrounding them came to a head.

Less than five weeks after the season had ended, and one month away from the 10-year anniversary of the team's inception, then-Predators owner Craig Leipold announced his intentions to sell the team to Canadian businessman Jim Balsillie.

With ownership up in the air and no clear indication that the Predators would actually be playing hockey in Nashville for the 2007–08 season, the team experienced what could only be described as a fire sale. Star players Paul Kariya and Peter Forsberg wouldn't be back, the latter recovering from foot surgery while Kariya opted to become a free agent.

"The whole situation is difficult. Our team is for sale, our payroll has to be a lot lower. The franchise is fighting for its life. This is a tough time here in Nashville," Poile told the media at the time.

His job growing increasingly more difficult and his roster falling apart outside the control of his hands, Poile jettisoned long-time players Tomas Vokoun, Kimmo Timonen, and Scott Hartnell, all of whom had played the entirety of their careers with the Predators.

As Poile continued to try and stop the bleeding from a payroll perspective, it was a wait-and-see moment for the organization throughout the remainder of the summer.

After receiving help from the local fanbase rallying to save the organization and after Leipold reneged on his letter of agreement to sell the team to Balsillie, Nashville acquired a new ownership group loyal to keeping the team in town as well as committed to growing the franchise.

"With the ownership changes to that point, there was some doubt that started with players that didn't re-sign here," said Poile. "It's with your sponsors that aren't as committed as you'd like your sponsors to be, and it certainly tests the loyalty of your fans. Support was good, but it wasn't great. The Predators were popular, but it wasn't over the top. We were doing ok, but ok's not good in anybody's books."

The damage was done. The Predators had lost some of their brightest stars while struggling to replace them during the fluid period of the ownership situation. Key forwards like J.P. Dumont, Jason Arnott, Alexander Radulov, Martin Erat, and David Legwand remained, but the team would need plenty of help across the board to remain as competitive as they had been in the previous two seasons—collecting 216 points in that span, fifth-most in the NHL.

Nashville began the 2007–08 on a successful note, winning its first two games of the season against the Colorado Avalanche and Dallas Stars by a combined score of 9–1. Goaltender Chris Mason stopped 63 of 64 shots and Legwand recorded a hat trick in the game against the Stars.

The wheels fell off quickly after that.

The Predators finished the month of October, which included the next nine games, on a 2–7–0 losing stretch. Mason was in goal for all seven of the losses, with goaltender Dan Ellis stepping in for the two wins, against the Atlanta Thrashers and Florida Panthers.

Nashville would be outscored 37–17 during the nine-game stretch, also going 0–19 on the power play through five of those nine games.

The wheels then abruptly re-attached themselves to the bus for the month of November, when Predators

Jordin Tootoo was a fan-favorite during his time with Nashville for his devastating checks and how quickly he dropped the gloves with opponents.

rebounded for an 8–2–2 month to bring their record to 12–9–2 through the first two months of the season.

Mason and Ellis were swapping duties in net, giving the Preds a solid one-two punch at goaltender without overworking either.

Offensively, things were clicking for Nashville as well.

Erat, Dumont, Legwand, and Radulov all contributed to the Predators' offense, as did players like Radek Bonk, Martin Gelinas, Vernon Fiddler, and the heavy-hitting Jordin Tootoo.

With the lack of a serious punch behind the offense that Nashville had in the previous two seasons, head coach Barry Trotz had to utilize a scoring-by-committee approach—one that would become a staple of his coaching career with the Predators for the next handful of years afterwards.

As the 2007 calendar year wound down, Nashville found themselves dead last in the Central Division and fourth-worst in the Western Conference at 18–18–2, good for a measly 38 points.

"The vultures were circling," said Neil McCormack, a former Predators season ticket holder and currently a writer's assistant on NBC's *Chicago Fire*. "It felt that the whole of the NHL was awaiting, even hoping, for a failure in Nashville."

It would be an improbable climb out of the cellar for Nashville, which was five points behind Anaheim for the final playoff spot in the Western Conference, but with Chicago, Columbus, and St. Louis all ahead of them in the division fighting for that final playoff spot as well.

Conference games, as well as divisional games, were even more important going into the second half of the season.

Ellis and Mason continued to guide the Predators as the month of January began, which included a home-and-home sweep against the Blues.

Nashville was starting to piece together wins and climb themselves back into the Western Conference playoff picture.

With a 4–2 win over the Blue Jackets on January 31st, the Predators leap-frogged over Columbus to slide into the eighth and final playoff spot—moving up to second in the Central, 23 points behind the dominant Red Wings.

Nashville had to hold onto the spot for the next 30 games to secure themselves a fourth-straight trip to the postseason. After all the events leading up to the season, the Predators were succeeding when everyone seemed to be expecting them to flounder.

"All of the turmoil of the team ownership and the uncertainty seemed to solidify that team," Amy Dunnavant, former season ticket holder, said. "Back then, I felt like we had a playoff team that could compete."

By the end of February, the Predators would continue to hang on to the final Western Conference playoff spot—tied with Colorado at 72 points, but pulling ahead of the other three teams below them in the Central.

If the first two months of 2008 were any indication, the home stretch proved to be just as important as what Nashville had done to that point in the season.

Losing six of the first 10 games of March left the Predators with just a two-point gap between them and the ninth-place Phoenix Coyotes, with the Blackhawks and Blue Jackets only three points behind as well.

Seven games remained for Nashville to close out the season—all against divisional opponents: two against the Blue Jackets, two against the Blues, and one against Detroit, all bookended by games against the Blackhawks.

It was a gauntlet if the Predators had ever seen one, a Murderer's Row between them and a playoff spot against undoubtedly the Red Wings.

Ellis had taken over much of the starts in net for the Preds through the month of March, and it would primarily be up to him to guide Nashville back to the playoffs.

March 22nd through the 28th, the Predators would take the first three games of the final seven, beating

Chicago in a shootout and seeing Ellis post back-to-back shutouts against Columbus. It would place Nashville in a three-way tie with the Edmonton Oilers and Vancouver Canucks for the final two playoff spots in the West.

Following a shutout loss to Detroit, Nashville would head to St. Louis to begin their final three games of the year—the first two being a home-and-home series against the Blues with four crucial points up for grabs.

With Ellis in net, Nashville went on to surrender three straight goals through the first 6:46 of the first period. Ellis was yanked in favor of Mason, who had to turn the net into a brick wall as the Predators were left with a huge hole to climb out of.

A goal from Nashville forward Brandon Bochenski midway through the second period got the ball rolling. Tootoo and Fiddler evened things up in the third period.

Less than two minutes into overtime, Rich Peverley notched the fourth unanswered goal for the Predators, securing two all-important points. It would be back to Nashville for a meeting against this same Blues team in just two days.

On the morning of April 3rd, with two games left to play, the Preds were one point ahead of Vancouver for the final spot in the West. Both teams were scheduled to play that evening, with Nashville's game ending right as Vancouver was to begin.

Two points that evening for the Predators, and a loss by the Canucks, would secure them a playoff spot.

"The stakes were so much higher than just a post-season berth," said McCormack. "This team had been stripped to the bone. This fanbase had been told they weren't worthy of a franchise. Everyone's emotions were running high, and the building was ripe with anticipation."

"I was very nervous," said season ticket holder Jeremy Sargent. "There had been games earlier in the year where we would try to snatch defeat from the jaws of victory. We had to win this game and hope [Vancouver] lost to get into the playoffs."

The game began much like any other would. After the puck dropped, both St. Louis and Nashville traded opportunities, trying to find a chink in the other's armor. It wasn't until midway through the first period that Jerred Smithson batted a puck out of midair past Blues goaltender Hannu Toivonen while shorthanded to give the Predators an all-important 1–0 lead.

"I'm glad I listened to my father," Smithson said to media after the game. "He always told me to go for a line drive in baseball instead of swinging for a home run."

Early in the second period, Blues forward Jay McClement tied the game. Not four minutes later, David Backes gave St. Louis the lead.

For the second straight game against them, Nashville would have to come from behind to beat the Blues.

With 2:14 left in the second period, Dumont lasered a shot past Toivonen to tie the game at two. That's how the game stayed going into the third.

Nashville had to find a way to pull the game out. Without it, the playoff aspirations for that season could go up like a puff of smoke.

"I remember my friend and I being pretty nervous," said Predators fan Michael Herndon. "The stakes were obviously very high and the game had been very evenly matched up to that point. It really felt like the smallest thing could tip the balance either way."

St. Louis gained possession as the third period began and took it right into the offensive zone, sending a shot toward Ellis barely a minute in. The Predators then re-grouped and focused on trying to keep the puck out and toward Toivonen.

Battling deep into the Blues' end, defenseman Eric Brewer collected the puck along the far boards and attempted to dump it back to the neutral zone. Jan Hlavac stopped it before it escaped and sent it back behind the St. Louis net, where Dumont would grabbed the puck, subsequently lost his footing, and dished the puck out to the slot in hopes a Predators player would find it.

Defenseman Greg de Vries did and wristed a shot past Toivonen for a 3–2 Nashville lead.

Now they'd just have to hold the lead for another 16 minutes. Easy street, right?

"They spent the rest of the period mostly trying to keep the Blues from equalizing," said Herndon. "You could feel how bad the team wanted to hold on for the victory. They were blocking shots, diving for pucks, and generally playing desperate hockey. The more effort the players gave, the more the crowd began to be whipped in to a frenzy.

"By the final TV timeout, most of the arena was on their feet."

The Blues would out-attempt Nashville with shots 5–1 over the next five minutes. As the game grew closer to the final horn, however, the noise level slowly built throughout the arena and continued at a steady pace.

Fans in Nashville, who had nearly lost their team 10 months prior, were finally feeling a sense of accomplishment for the team they banded together to save—as some forget that many in the ownership group who purchased the team were fans prior to doing so.

"Ever since the potential sale of the team, the fans' relationship with the team changed," said Predators season ticket holder Kathy Lenhart. "There is so much connection and feeling of involvement with this team that is hard to explain."

In 2007, Predators fans started their own tradition of a standing ovation during TV timeouts, a tradition that continues today.

With 4:30 left to go in the third period, Toivonen froze the puck off a Radulov wrist shot and the game went to the final TV timeout of the evening. All the feverous noise Predators fans had been exuding over the past handful of minutes had finally reached a breaking point.

"The TV timeout began, and like any usual timeout, we paused to let the crowd cheer a bit before we jumped into doing a PA promotion, or what happened to be scheduled during that break," said Predators Game

Presentation Coordinator Ron Zolkower. "As we paused for the usual breather, the crowd became louder and louder. At that point, Brian Campbell [Director of Game Presentation] made the call to just let the crowd take it as long as they could and that lasted the entire two-minute commercial break."

Through the entire timeout, fans stood on their feet—waving free t-shirts that had been given away for the home finale—and raising the decibel level to one that likely hadn't been felt in that arena since the first playoff game a handful of seasons ago.

"It was pretty organic across the arena, but I know a lot of us in The Cellblock were up and screaming right away," said Predators season ticket holder Mark Hollingsworth, who goes by the moniker "The Warden" of section 303—known as The Cellblock and home to fans that normally start much of the chants during home games. "It just felt like it *had* to be done. I held up my sign that says, 'We play hockey LOUD!' and it was shown on the Megatron, which helped spur the crowd even further.

"We've heard since 1998 how players feed off the amazing energy of Smashville. And, honestly, I think when the fans roar like that, it becomes self-fulfilling prophecy for *us* as well—it just keeps us fully engaged—like we are *all* part of making it happen on the ice."

The Predators battled through the remaining handful of minutes of regulation and picked up their final win of the 2007–08 regular season, beating St. Louis 3–2. Hours later, Edmonton defeated Vancouver 2–1—securing Nashville's spot in the playoffs and a second meeting in four seasons with the Red Wings.

Players marveled after the game of the energy level coursing through the building from the fans.

"That was huge," Ellis said. "We were able to feed off of that. It gave us a lot of energy to get us through the final minutes."

Trotz would marvel at it as well, and how it interfered with his coaching abilities.

"If you are standing behind the bench it is pretty impressive to look at the community and the people in the stands," said Trotz after the game. "It was pretty loud on the bench because I was trying to call lines and the guys couldn't hear me."

Nashville's public address announcer Paul McCann, who also runs his own personal Predators blog on the popular hockey blogging platform HockeyBuzz.com, summed up the entire event afterwards as succinctly as possible:

A palpable buzz ran through the rink as game time approached and when the team hit the ice, the denizens of Pred Nation welcomed their team with one of the loudest ovations I have heard the arena in quite a while . . . it was a roar that would seem relatively quiet compared to what was to come.

The game followed a familiar script, solid first period, early lead, flat beginning to the second period, give up the lead, get their legs back under them, come back for a third period lead, hang on for the win. Pred Nation has seen this movie before . . . however . . .

Each period has three planned TV timeouts . . . they happen at the first whistle after 14 minutes, 10 minutes, and 6 minutes. When the whistle blew at 4:36 remaining, the crowd began to cheer their appreciation for their team . . . the game day crew had a video tribute to play during the TV timeout, and we waited for the cheer to subside.

It didn't . . .

I never got to introduce that video . . . That cheer just grew louder as the entire arena stood up . . . and grew louder as fans began to wave their free t-shirts . . . and grew louder as the team bench was shown on the MegaTron.

That standing ovation filled the entire 2-minute TV timeout and even spilled over into the next 30 seconds of game play . . .

It was Pred Nation saying thank you to the team . . . It was Pred Nation saying thank you to the new ownership . . . thank you to the folks who worked so hard to keep their team in Nashville . . . and a small bit was Pred Nation giving the finger to anyone who dared suggest that hockey does not belong in Nashville.

Things could have gone much worse for Nashville with so much at stake for the organization.

Had the Predators been unable to find a way to tie the game and then take the lead in the third period, perhaps even losing the game, Nashville could've found itself out of the playoffs altogether.

Having nothing to play for, Vancouver lost 7–1 to Calgary two days later, and Nashville dropped its season finale as well in Chicago the very next night after beating St. Louis—two crucial points at the end of the season that could have been a huge factor in determining whether the Predators would make the playoffs had they lost to the Blues.

That wasn't how it was to go down, however. Predators fans started something back in 2008 that they continue to perform a decade later, whenever they feel

Predators players and coaches often give Nashville's fans plenty of accolades for the energy that surges through Bridgestone Arena on game nights.

the team needs a lift on the ice or maybe just a congratulatory ovation.

It's just another part of what makes the Predators one of the more unique organizations across the NHL and what makes them Smashville.

Chapter Thirteen

Being Traded: Life from a Player's Perspective

Just as contract talks are a major part of the business that is professional hockey, so too are trades. They happen all the time and, regardless of how it personally impacts a player, these are primarily made as business decisions to better the organization.

Sometimes, a player is fully aware that they're going to be traded, either by initiating the trade conversations themselves or through contact from the team's general manager prior to a trade being sought out.

On the opposite end of the spectrum, players can and will be traded with no or minimal prior knowledge to the situation. Most times players have an inkling that they're at least on the trade block, but even so it can be a shock to the system to get that fateful call that your entire life is about to be uprooted.

"We had been in Toronto for almost four years at that time," said defenseman Cody Franson, who started his career in Nashville before being sent to Toronto and then traded back to the Preds early in 2015. "I would have liked to have stayed [in Toronto], but at the time they were kind of in the midst of not really knowing exactly what they wanted to do in terms of rebuilding or signing guys. We had a couple of brief conversations in terms of contract talks but nothing too committal, so I had the feeling that I might get traded because they didn't want to just lose me if they weren't going to sign me.

"When I got the trade call, it didn't really surprise me. It did surprise me that it was to Nashville. I had had some conversations with [Dave Nonis, former general manager of the Maple Leafs] at that time and we had a great relationship. He knew I loved it in Toronto and would like to have played there for a lot longer, but there's certain things that they had to do from an organizational standpoint and they were able to get a good return."

From a managerial perspective, many of these deals often hinge upon what the return is as opposed to what the team is trading away. If a team knows it may not be in the playoffs that season, they're likely to be dubbed "sellers" and will part ways with players—many times, those with expiring contracts—to teams in better positions in the standings, known as "buyers."

Sometimes, it's for the best. Franson was traded in the latter half of the 2015 season, along with another former Predators player in Mike Santorelli as well as Olli Jokinen and Brendan Leipsic, to Nashville for a first-round selection in the upcoming draft that summer.

That first-round pick was subsequently traded to the Philadelphia Flyers prior to being used, and the Flyers would select forward Travis Konecny.

Most trades that are made across the NHL have multiple pieces tied to them. Rarely do you see a one-for-one player trade executed where both teams are happy with the end result long-term.

In Nashville's case, the team made two such trades in the same year. The summer of 2016 saw the Predators deal Shea Weber to Montreal for P.K. Subban, a seismic shift heard around the hockey world. Nearly six months prior, they'd make equally as impressive of a splash, sending defenseman Seth Jones to the Columbus Blue Jackets in return for top center Ryan Johansen.

For Johansen, it was an interesting process to undertake.

"I was on the trade block that year," Johansen said when asked about his initial thoughts on being traded for the first time in his career. "I was only informed by my agent if there were talks or things that may have been talked about with myself and my future in Columbus or moving somewhere. All I heard was a few things from my agent and then just the rumors that you'd hear about or people would text you about things like that.

"You really don't have an exact idea of what's going on. It was interesting. That was the first time I had been traded in my life, so it was an interesting process in how it went down, and how your life changes kind of instantly and you're on a plane heading to a new chapter, so it was interesting."

There are even rarer occasions where more than two teams are involved in exchanging different players. Maybe Team A wants a player on Team B but Team C has the draft pick that Team B wants. It happens from time to time, not as often as a normal trade and even rarer than a one-for-one player trade, but it can be fascinating to see it all unfold.

In one example, Nashville had been high on trying to acquire forward Matt Duchene from the Colorado Avalanche. As high on him as the Preds were, Poile never found a trade package that would work to pry Duchene away.

Enter the Ottawa Senators.

With Senators management unable to find common ground in re-signing center Kyle Turris, they were able to find a solution.

The Predators would send highly-touted defensive Samuel Girard, forward prospect Vladislav Kamenev, and a 2018 second-round pick to the Avalanche. Colorado passed Duchene over to the Senators. Ottawa sent Turris back to Nashville.

Everyone was happy.

How quickly would Turris hear from the Predators after the trade was executed?

"Pretty much immediately," said Turris, recalling the day of the trade. "I talked to [Poile] basically immediately after. I talked to a bunch of people in the organization that night and guys on the team, and yeah, just everybody welcoming me right away."

Both Franson and Johansen can relate, as each was called by the general manager for the team for which they had played, as well as the general manager for the team to which they were heading—sometimes, only hours apart.

"Both times I got traded I heard from the GM," Franson said. "When I got traded to Toronto I heard from Mr. Poile. When I got traded to Nashville, I heard from Mr. Nonis, and then I spoke to my agent after that phone call."

"I think it was [Columbus general manager Jarmo Kekäläinen] who called me and then they were all down at the Nationwide Arena and I went in to see them," said Johansen. "We had a fifteen- or twenty-minute conversation about everything, a good talk with those guys and closed that all out.

"I think [Poile] called me that night, but for sure I saw him the next morning at like seven or eight a.m. I had to go through the physical process and go to the doctors to be cleared and then I made my way down to the rink here where he met me earlier and had a conversation about everything."

When it comes to being sent to a new city, especially one in which a player doesn't have much experience, it's always helpful when there's someone on the other end to guide you in that process. Largely, the general manager of the incoming team will take the reins and at least offer up basic knowledge to the player, or put him in touch with some of his new teammates who can help further.

Poile has tried to make the process as seamless as possible for anyone transitioning to the Predators organization, and just as so on the way out.

"Right away it was 'Welcome to the organization. We're excited to have you. How's your family doing?'" said Turris. "[Poile] explained Nashville to me and the city and the organization. He's a very personable person. He's very nice, very genuine and welcoming, and made me feel comfortable and excited right away, and then went into the process of 'ok, we have to get your work visa next' and the logistics of everything.

"He and everybody in the organization and on the team here have made me feel comfortable and helped make the transition a lot easier than it could have been."

Even as helpful as a GM like Poile can be, sometimes it takes additional support to transition most smoothly.

"My now-fiancée made it an easy transition because it would have been a scramble if I was by myself,"

Johansen said, laughing as he recalled the moments after he had been traded. "I just quickly packed a couple of bags and I flew out that night. I think I was traded around like seven o'clock and I was on a plane by nine-thirty or ten heading down to Nashville, so I packed a couple of bags quick and she ended up packing up my whole place in Columbus and moved everything down to Nashville, where we moved into an apartment and started with our new team and city here."

Not all trades are perfect, however. Even when a trade brings back a player such as Franson, one who began his career in Nashville, it may not necessarily be a match made in heaven.

Given Franson's previous history with the Predators and the fact that he was already available on the trade block, he was a logical choice for Poile to bring back into the fold. However, Nashville's defensive needs in 2015 didn't exactly call for another right-handed shot on the roster.

"When they first traded for me, they had [Ryan] Ellis, [Seth] Jones, and Weber on their right-hand side," said Franson. "I didn't really understand why they wanted to bring me in. They didn't need power-play guys. I was having a good year in Toronto going into [unrestricted free agency]. I loved going back there. I was really comfortable there. I was playing with guys that I knew and that whole comfort transition was great, but as far as fitting into their needs in the lineup, I was really anxious about that when they made the trade for me.

"I was really hopeful that it would work out because I love it there, but I was anxious about it and unfortunately my worries kind of came true. Asking Jones to try and play the left side isn't always an easy thing to do for a right-handed defenseman, so that didn't really work. Jones was obviously a great player already at that time and Ellis was starting to play really well. He had been playing well at that time and obviously Weber is Weber. That's three right-handed shots that are all power-play guys. It ended up not being a good fit and that's probably the most unfortunate circumstance I had in Nashville."

Franson would contribute one goal and three assists in 23 games after returning to Nashville—not including his two assists in five playoff games.

With his contract expiring after the season ended, Franson hit free agency and found himself heading to the Buffalo Sabres on a two-year deal, before then signing with the Chicago Blackhawks prior to the start of the 2017–18 season.

He ended the year playing in the AHL with the Rockford Ice Hogs.

There's no telling where he would have ended up had he finished his year in Toronto and then hit free agency.

"I love it in Nashville. I still have a great respect for the people there," Franson said. "The people there treated me great. That'll always be my first home in this league. It's always fun going back, you know, even with the way things shook out the last time I was there. But when you ask if I'd rather stay in Toronto, I think that probably would've been much better for my career.

"I was having a really good year and playing in situations that were good for me. I was on the first unit power play playing over twenty minutes a night and being put in situations that I could be successful in, and going into free agency I think things probably would have went differently for me had I stayed in Toronto."

General managers have their work cut out for them, especially when it comes to the trade market. At the end of the day, the NHL is, first and foremost, a business.

Chapter Fourteen

The Greatest General Manager

It's not often that you come across an individual who can have such a lasting impact on a business, city, and community like that of Predators general manager David Poile.

Since 1972, Poile has been in and around an NHL front office. He's helped to shape two separate NHL franchises, starting with the Washington Capitals in 1982, until he departed for the Music City in 1997.

When Poile arrived in Nashville, he didn't plan on it being a short layover until his next job.

"My goal was that this would be my last job," said Poile. "Having said that, coming in here at age forty-eight, I was hoping that I was going to have some longevity. When I was at my press conference when I was hired by Washington, for some reason I said 'I'm not here for a good time, I'm here for a long time.' I don't know why I said that. You know what I mean, you have certain goals that I have, written goals and things like that, and some of them longevity is important. My plan wasn't to be here three or four years. I'll put it that way."

Since day one, Poile has meticulously crafted the Predators to his design—hiring only two head coaches in that span as well as keeping the bulk of the hockey operations staff largely in place for the same amount of time.

What does it take, though, to be a successful manager in the NHL? Even through a series of ownership changes with Nashville, Poile was able to ride the waves and keep his ship steady towards the end goal.

"I think it's the whole organization. You have to hire the right people and the right position and everybody has to do their job," Poile noted. "What I've found specifically with this franchise in the early part is we weren't necessarily always on the same page. We had some strengths and we had some weaknesses. We had three ownership changes and whenever that happens you, for the reasons when the team was sold, can't be on the same page so something is going to suffer.

"It's going to be hard to be successful. [2018] is an easier time to talk about because now it feels I know we're on the same page: the business side, the hockey side, the ownership, and we're all going in the same direction both on and off the ice. You have to make sure that you hire the right people and make sure that they know their job and that they do their job and then look at it globally as an organizational thing that you need everybody to be working in the same direction. It starts with the ownership, goes to the hockey ops, goes to the business side, so it's a combination of a lot of things."

Outside of surrounding himself with the right people, Poile also had to make the right moves on the ice to keep his team competitive in one of, if not the most, competitive divisions in all of the NHL.

The Central Division has been the home of the Nashville Predators since the team joined the league for the 1998–99 season. Seeing teams like the Detroit Red Wings, Chicago Blackhawks, and St. Louis Blues as mainstays in the first years of the franchise, Poile had his work cut out for him in order to stay within reaching distance of some of the league's best, but he's never shied away from the prospect of making a deal to better his team—even if it involves dealing with his direct competition.

It's one of the most crucial elements in being a successful general manager. The right trade can be the final puzzle piece to push a team over the top on their way to winning a Stanley Cup championship. Contextually, trading Seth Jones for Ryan Johansen has been one deal that has set both the Columbus Blue Jackets and the Predators on a greater path for success.

"I know I was trying to think of any other way not to [trade Seth Jones]," lamented Poile. "When you talk about puzzle pieces, that was the fit for them and Johansen was the fit for us, so it made sense and it seems to be working great for both teams."

Conversely, the wrong trade—and this seemingly happens more often than not—can disrupt team chemistry on and off the ice as well as push a team further away from long-term success.

One thing for which many praise Poile is his saint-like patience to wait out his opposition when making a deal, never truly overpaying for talent when the right offer comes his way.

"The whole key is preparation in knowing what you're looking for. I'll have a hundred conversations, maybe more, on trading for every deal that you'll make," says Poile.

"In the last three years we've had the concerted effort with total focus both in drafting and making acquisitions to get more offensive forwards and specifically [centers] when the opportunity presented itself. If you see what we've done in the last two or three years, our center ice has totally changed where now we have [Ryan Johansen]; [Kyle Turris]; [Nick Bonino]; [Calle Jarnkrok], who was in the minors like three years ago; and [Colton Sissons], who was either being drafted or in the minors. That's what we really felt that we needed. You've got to be prepared and know what you want to get."

"Also, acquiring assets, even though they might be a duplication somewhere, might serve you well another time," Poile continued. "Drafting Seth Jones is probably a good example of that. It's not like we wanted to trade Seth Jones, but we needed a [center] more than we needed another top-four defenseman."

Sometimes a trade can take multiple years to come to fruition. Is that not the best way to define patience? Poile has been willing to wait to make sure the right trade is made to better the Predators.

A prime example? Forward Kyle Turris. His trade to Nashville was a continual work-in-progress for over a year, and Poile didn't even get the player he was initially trying to get.

"An example just recently is the [Matt] Duchene three-way deal," said Poile. "I mean, we've been talking about Duchene for I think a year, year and a half. We didn't get Duchene, but from that was the same principle, of trying to get a [center], that we ended up getting Turris. That took a long time."

Before all the trades, a team had to be built. Poile was instrumental in constructing Nashville's on-ice talent from the ground up, starting with the 1998 Expansion Draft. Since the Predators had their day plucking players off of rosters across the league, there have been three other

David Legwand, Nashville's first-ever draft selection, played 956 of his 1136 total games in the NHL for the Predators.

Expansion Drafts for new teams: the Atlanta Thrashers (now Winnipeg Jets), the Columbus Blue Jackets, and the Las Vegas Golden Knights.

All three teams prior to Las Vegas experienced stringent policies in terms of who they could draft and who pre-existing teams could protect. Had Nashville, Atlanta, and Columbus had the resources available to draft that the Golden Knights had prior to the 2017–18 season, there might have been quicker success across the board.

"There's no 'maybe' in that," reflected Poile, who appeared a bit agitated when looking back at his expansion draft compared to that of Las Vegas. "The way I always answer that is 'hats off to the NHL for getting it right' and good job by Vegas, but with all due respect, I don't think the NHL did right by the previous expansion teams going all the way to the first expansion.

"They allowed the current teams to protect way too many players. They didn't give any expansion team an opportunity to be successful at the beginning, and because of that, I think there was a lot of time and money wasted getting these teams up to snuff. I mean, managers got fired, coaches got fired, teams got sold, teams got transferred, and the Vegas model is the correct model."

Now being on the flip-side of the Expansion Draft equation for the third time, and potentially more if the NHL expands further, it's understood that sometimes you're going to have to give up a great player. Nashville lost James Neal to the Golden Knights in the most recent expansion, the first time they were to give up a player, as they were protected from doing so in 1999 and 2000 both.

From a general manager's point of view, it's harrowing to know that no matter what you do, no matter how many trades you try to make to increase your level of protection, you're still bound to lose a great player from your organization.

"It'll be interesting in the next expansion time around how people do it because a lot of people didn't take their poison," said Poile. "They traded like a first pick or they traded a younger player or something like that where we just took our poison, so to speak, and we allowed [Las Vegas] to take James Neal with the idea and hope that a Colton Sissons or a Calle Jarnkrok can come in and develop.

"This is all part and parcel of your cap. There's many ways to look at it, but arguably if we still had Neal—who's a great player and I'm not saying we wanted to lose him—we'd probably be in no position cap-wise to get [Kyle Turris]. You just never know how it's going to work out but it's painful now because, you know, we saw what happened in Vegas. We know it's going to be the same if it's Seattle or the next team that comes in, we're going to lose a good player. It's going to be painful."

Painful, yes, but the bigger question is how do you prevent that if you can? Most teams and general managers have the ability to try to make an arrangement with the expansion team—whether it's trading an extra draft pick here or there in lieu of selecting a certain player that's been left exposed.

The greatest struggle for most, though, is trying to prognosticate how a team will look whenever the next expansion draft happens.

"It's really hard to do that," Poile said. "You could do a ghost protected list or what have you, but you know if you're competing at a high level, I guess that we're certainly not going to sell off a player to get a player that could be exempt or what have you. I'd say that's going to be, we'll be aware of it. We'll know what we're going to be losing approximately, but I mean, I guess there could be circumstances that could change that.

"If you trade away somebody for futures to put yourself in a better position. I guess if you're a non-playoff team in that year you could do some things like these teams are doing at the deadline to get futures and get some of your non-exempt players off of there. Sort of lessen the burden."

Poile has had the prowess of drafting some of the best players, especially when it comes to defensemen, in the NHL. In full retrospect, Poile, along with the help of his scouting staff, selected players like Ryan Suter, Kevin Klein, and Shea Weber all in one draft, found Pekka Rinne in the eighth round, Patric Hornqvist in the seventh, as well as both Craig Smith and Mattias Ekholm in the fourth.

There have also been picks that may not have been the best: taking goaltender Brian Finley sixth overall in 1999 and drafting defenseman Ryan Parent in 2005 ahead of other defensemen such as Marc-Edouard Vlasic and Kris Letang.

Hindsight, though, is always 20/20. Any GM would love to have a mulligan to use at one point in their career.

"You always look at who you drafted and why and if that was the right thing to the guys that you didn't draft and why," noted Poile. "I think we self-critique all the time with what we learn from that and players that you could've had available or traded that, you know, you didn't think were that good. I think that's a continual exercise, but again that goes back to being prepared and evaluating your players correctly which sometimes, you know, we overvalue our own players.

"Timing is such a big factor in any business, but for hockey it certainly is, it's when you make the move and who you make the move for and what you make the move for. They say if you hit .300 in baseball you're in the Hall of Fame. Everybody's got things they wish they could do better or things they wish they hadn't done, but hopefully we're hitting on a lot more good things than things that we would regret."

After two disappointing losses in the playoffs to the San Jose Sharks in 2006 and 2007, Nashville returned to the postseason in 2008, finishing second again in the Central Division, but fell short during the subsequent 2008–09 season. It would be the first time the team had missed the playoffs in the previous five seasons.

Offensively, Nashville just didn't appear to be the same team anymore. The fire sale had taken its toll on the roster, while fan support of the team was arguably at an all-time low. The Predators struggled most nights, on and off the ice. It may have been different had their third-leading scorer from the previous season remained with the team.

But it was not to be. Alexander Radulov—who had finished his second full season for the Preds with 58 points in 81 games—was tearing up the fledgling KHL in Russia, halfway across the world. Meanwhile, the 2009 Preds hovered around the .500 mark for the first five months of the season.

But why was he in the KHL in the first place? Poile wouldn't let one of his draftees, especially one as talented as Radulov, just head back home to play with the NHL's leading competitor, would he?

For one of the few times in his storied career, Poile had to watch as one of the most talented players to ever be drafted by the Predators walked away from the team on his own accord. It was an unprecedented situation that would cause an international uproar.

With one year remaining on his initial entry-level contract after being drafted by Nashville, Radulov signed a three-year deal with Salavat Yulaev Ufa during the summer of 2008.

"I told my bosses in Nashville that I wanted to play at home and some Russian clubs were offering me much better conditions than I had in Nashville," Radulov told the Russian media at the time.

"They said they would call me back but never phoned. It seems that they were either not really interested in me or just did not believe I could return home. One way or another, I'm happy to come home."

Poile and the Predators, however, believed that this signed contract wouldn't be an issue for them. In addition, they believed that Radulov would be in Nashville for the start of training camp as if nothing had changed.

"Alex is under contract with the Nashville Predators through the 2008–09 season. We are looking forward to him being here for training camp and being a part of this franchise's success for years to come," said Poile in a press release sent out after Radulov's KHL contract signing.

Nashville, along with backing from the NHL and the IIHF, went on to argue that Radulov's contract obligated him to play with the Predators, at least through the 2009 season. The KHL, on the opposite end, argued that the Radulov deal was valid as he signed with Salavat Yulaev five days prior to the international transfer agreement being signed by both the NHL and KHL.

The back and forth continued. Radulov was suspended without pay by the Predators for the 2008–09 season on September 2nd.

It would be three full years before he would return to Nashville, when the Predators would be contending for the Stanley Cup. And much like how thunder follows lightning, controversy continued to follow Radulov in Nashville.

In the early-morning hours prior to Game Two against the Phoenix Coyotes in the 2012 Stanley Cup Playoffs, both Radulov and fellow winger Andrei Kostitsyn were spotted out and about, missing curfew in the process.

The pair were suspended for the third and fourth games of the series, which Nashville would ultimately lose in five. Game Five marked the final time Radulov donned a Predators sweater.

In hindsight, Poile noted that there could have been some things done differently with regard to Radulov.

"It's high maintenance," said Poile, referring to his relationship with Radulov. "There's probably two sides to that story, too. He [was] a young player. Our philosophy has been, for the most part, 'the road to Nashville is through Milwaukee,' and, you know, we probably didn't get off to a good start with him because he went down there and got, what, five or six points in the first couple of games and he's still down there and, you know, maybe we should have started him. Again, there was opportunities.

"There was money—different money that you could make here versus there, and just different things. He was young and he had some, what do you want to call it, just growing up to do. Maybe we could have done a couple of things different. Maybe he could have done a couple of things different. We got a really good player and a dynamic player, an exciting player that was going to put up some offense and it didn't work out as well as we could have hoped for."

The Predators, as is often the case, continued to stay resilient. It may have taken some time, but the on-ice product eventually began to right itself at the turn of the decade.

All the while Poile continued to mold the Predators into a world-class team. Outside of Nashville though, he would try to put his own unique stamp on the league, becoming one of the inaugural members of the NHL's Competition Committee—a long-standing position he's held since the committee's creation in 2005.

One of the many changes the committee has issued? Coach's Challenge and the video review system. Both were products that would become eventualities in a league that hadn't utilized such systems in the past. One could have been a direct result of a game featuring the Predators.

"There's always been tweaks to the game. I don't think any of us are trying to reinvent the game," Poile said. "It's maybe making the game faster with less interference, less hooking. Our job is sort of to be the guardians of the game. That's why we have [Competition Committee] meetings. We may not make any changes, but, believe me, we talk about a lot of different things.

"Say you have a power play, you get to choose which side [of the ice] you want it on, meaning our strongest guys are right-handed guys so we would like it on the right side. Right now, it's where the goalie or where the play stops or whatever. I'm not saying to do that, I'm just giving you something that's [currently] worth talking about."

Back in February of 2013, forward Matt Duchene, then of the Colorado Avalanche, collected a loose puck at the blue line while positioned at least two feet ahead of it en route to scoring a goal against then-Predators goaltender Chris Mason. Most, if not all, of Nashville's players and coaching staff thought the play would be whistled offside—as it should have been, to which upon reviewing the replay even the Avalanche television broadcast crew agreed to.

The play, however, was waved forward, and Duchene raced in and put the puck past Mason to give the Avalanche a 3–1 lead at the time. Colorado would end up winning 6–5 and the Predators would lose five of their next seven games.

"I wasn't happy when I was watching TV," recollected Poile. "I called the War Room right away. It's like you pick up the phone and they say 'We know. We know.'"

Three seasons later, the league voted to allow for coaches to challenge goals scored, but in certain circumstances only. One of those circumstances included being offside, whether by an inch or a foot. To most, it's not perfect, but it's plays like the one involving Duchene and the Predators that Poile found indicative of a need for a discussion—even if it meant taking the new process to an extreme degree.

"[That play] got it going and unfortunately it got it going too far," Poile said. "We were looking for the egregious offside and now we've got it down to the foot in the air, which is too unfortunate but it is what it is. Overall the game is fine, I think the offside thing is actually accurate. You may not like the foot in the air, but it's accurate, so we don't have any problems with that anymore.

"You want to fix something that happens once every ten years and we are where we are. It's good the offside thing is there. We're not going to see any goals scored offside, I mean as painful as it might be for that little inch or foot, it's accurate."

Everything Poile does, whether for the league or for the Predators, is done in a meticulous fashion. He's never been one to shoot first and ask questions later, but more so one that will wait for the right opportunities to present themselves and act accordingly.

There's a reason that he stands as one of the longest-tenured general managers. He most recently earned the title of the winningest GM in NHL history, passing longtime Oilers and Rangers general manager Glen Sather.

It never ceases to amaze anymore whenever Poile makes a blockbuster deal or signs a key upcoming free agent to an amazing contract. What happens, though, when it's not just a normal trade, but for a player that was largely the face of the franchise at that point?

The day prior to the 2016 NHL Entry Draft, Poile took part in the annual general managers meeting—a normal occurrence on the day before the draft. From Anaheim to Winnipeg, general managers are seated alphabetically by their club. At the time, this would seat Poile in between Marc Bergevin of the Montreal Canadiens and Ray Shero of the New Jersey Devils.

Rumors had swirled in the weeks and months leading up to the draft that the Canadiens were far from happy with 2013 Norris Trophy-winning defenseman P.K. Subban, whose on-ice personality sometimes overshadowed his extraordinary talents. By Poile's account, the discussions with Bergevin took place as follows:

"Are you going to trade him?" Poile said to Bergevin during the meeting, not one to beat around the bush when it comes to business.

"I'm not trying to trade him," replied Bergevin.

"Well, that's not an answer. Are you going to trade him?" pushed Poile, trying to get a firmer stance.

"You never say never," Bergevin said, continuing to dodge the question.

Poile's ability to get a deal done, or not done, has always been one of patience, but this is a different beast entirely. This is P.K. Subban potentially up for trade, one of the game's top defensemen. You have to get either a yes or a no.

Being as straightforward as he could be, Poile offered up a simple six-word sentence—one that would grow to change the dynamic of both organizations:

"Do you want to do this?"

That was the beginning. Five days later, P.K. Subban was traded to the Predators, a one-for-one trade that sent Shea Weber back to Montreal.

"It was the only thing that was going to work," said Poile, reflecting back on the deal. "I mean, we can digest this in lots of different ways, but that was the only thing that we thought would work. [Bergevin] was saying he wasn't interested in a younger player or a first-round pick, so it was pretty obvious to me what the deal was."

Making the trade signified a changing of the guard for Nashville. Weber epitomized the Barry Trotz era: hard-nosed defense-first play while able to contribute offensively and play a 200-foot game. The Peter Laviolette-led Predators were turning a page and it was about what worked best for the team, not who the problem was.

In this case, trading for Subban—especially if he was available—was something Poile didn't think twice about pulling the trigger on.

"That's the toughest because you have to ask yourself 'Why?'" said Poile. "He wasn't the problem, but we're looking to be a little bit different. We hadn't won anything to that point. Skating and speed was where the game was going. [Subban]'s three and a half years younger than Shea, and again, that's the deal.

"I think it's going to be still years before it's told. They'll always be judged, you know, in such a big deal, but, I mean, both of these players have lots more to play in their careers, so it was time to do something of significance. That was all part and parcel of knowing what you want to do, knowing where you think your team is, or where it should be going. Where's the game going, and we did it."

That's how Poile runs his team. It's a chess game, except he's not just looking one or two moves in the future. He's playing a game or two ahead of the opponent, envisioning what will happen years from now instead of just months down the road.

No matter how long it continues for Nashville, Poile has easily solidified himself as one of the greatest general managers in NHL history. And rightfully so.

Chapter Fifteen

A History of
Hat Tricks

Scoring a hat trick in hockey, three goals all coming from the same player over the course of the contest, isn't something you see every day. For most teams, it's not as rare of a feat to register a hat trick as it is for the Predators.

Through the 2017–18 season, Nashville has recorded only 34 total hat tricks, including those scored in the post-season—just over a quarter of what the Edmonton Oilers had in the '80s alone (142). Granted, legendary forward Wayne Gretzky had 50 of those by himself, but it's still an incredible number.

That's not a slight at the Predators either, it's systematic of the changes to play league-wide. Scoring has become more difficult, as the rules have changed and talent has largely increased across the board.

From the 1991 expansion, which added the San Jose Sharks, through the end of the 2017–18 season, 10 expansion teams have combined for only 413 hat tricks total—an average of 41 per team.

Over one-third of Nashville's cumulative hat tricks (13) have been collected by players under the age of twenty-five. While it isn't entirely surprising, the fact that nearly half of those particular hat tricks were all scored by the same player, Filip Forsberg, is nevertheless a remarkable feat.

He's one of the Predators' most legitimate scoring threats they've had in franchise history. Currently, only former captain Jason Arnott (33, 2008–09) has scored as many goals in a season for Nashville that Forsberg has had (33, 2015–16). What's more incredible is the fact that Forsberg hasn't even reached his full potential yet, which most players historically do between the ages of twenty-six and twenty-eight.

Prior to a February 21st meeting against the Calgary Flames, Forsberg had notched a total of three hat tricks in his career—tying him with former Predators forward Scott Walker and setting him one behind Steve Sullivan for most all-time in franchise history.

Filip Forsberg has six as of the end of the 2017–18 season, two coming in back-to-back games during the 2015–16 season.

One of the more interesting hat tricks in Predators history, however, came courtesy of forward Eric Nystrom back in 2014. During a 5–4 shootout loss to the Calgary Flames, one of only five times in 34 games that Nashville had a player score a hat trick and then failed to win the game, Nystrom scored all four of Nashville's goals. As of 2018, Nystrom is the only player in Predators history to record four goals in a single game.

Nystrom was never a prolific scorer for the Predators, which made the bizarre outcome even more so. Not even Nystrom's father, longtime New York Islanders forward Bob Nystrom, scored four goals in a game during his career.

Of Nashville's 34 hat tricks, they've all come from players of varying ages and positions. Five of Forsberg's six hat tricks with the Predators all came before his twenty-third birthday, making him the youngest player in Predators history to record a hat trick.

It's not just limited to Nashville's young guns, though. At thirty-five years old, Steve Sullivan became one of only 71 players in NHL history to score three or more goals in a game at the age of thirty-five or older.

The aforementioned Nystrom and Sullivan, J.P. Dumont, Jason Arnott, Paul Kariya, Scott Walker, and Shea Weber are all part of the exclusive club of Predators to record a hat trick after passing the age of thirty.

Of them all, Weber's may be one of the most compelling hat tricks in franchise history, regardless if it came during a loss.

Against the Detroit Red Wings in December of 2015, Nashville took a 4–2 lead eight minutes into the third period thanks to Weber's third goal of the game. His hat trick was the first from a defenseman in franchise history. Unfortunately, Detroit would go on to score three unanswered goals, including the game-winner in overtime.

Weber's demeanor in his postgame press conferences has never been one of excitement, even in the best of outcomes. The loss, though, was Nashville's seventh in the previous nine at that point, so Weber was in no mood to reflect on the historic franchise milestone.

"[It doesn't feel] good right now, to tell you the truth," Weber said to reporters after the overtime loss.

Even in a loss, seeing a hat trick scored coming from either team is entertaining to watch. And Nashville fans have had more opportunities to see opposing players score a hat trick against the Predators than the opposite.

That may not be something to brag about, but there are some legends on that list, like Keith Tkachuk, Joe

Sakic, and Luc Robitaille. Nashville's seen its share of Predator-killers notch hat tricks as well, from Jarome Iginla and Jeff Skinner to Jeff Carter and Marian Gaborik.

In only a handful of seasons during their existence have the Predators had true goal-scorers at their disposal. Players like Kariya, Sullivan, James Neal and Forsberg aren't a dime a dozen for Nashville. They've never been a team to hover in the bottom five of the league year in and year out, bad enough to collect top draft picks and bring in talented young players through the NHL draft.

Three of the four players previously mentioned were acquired via trade, while Kariya was the only one who signed during the offseason in Nashville.

Maybe that stigma has changed for Nashville, especially after the run to the Stanley Cup Final in 2016–17.

What's a true certainty, though, is that Nashville will have plenty of talent to produce a plethora of goals in the immediate future. Who knows how many hat tricks will be added to the franchise totals ten, twenty, or even fifty years from now.

Chapter Sixteen

The Path to the Stanley Cup Final

When do you look at a season and start to believe it could be more special than all the others?

Nashville's 2016–17 season was one for the ages. It saw the Predators sneak into the playoffs as the NHL's final team and then run through the Western Conference like a buzzsaw on the path to the organization's first trip to the Stanley Cup Final.

It may have ended roughly 68 minutes too soon for the Preds, but it will still go down as the best season in Nashville's history. That is, until they lay claim to Lord Stanley's Cup itself.

For a year that had such an amazing finish to it, few saw it coming as the team worked its way through the final months of the 2016 calendar year.

Nashville had been transitioning from one of its wildest offseasons in franchise history, seeing the team trade captain Shea Weber for P.K. Subban back in June,

One of the NHL's most energetic players, defenseman P.K. Subban was traded to the Predators during the summer of 2016.

which sparked the debate as to whether general manager David Poile did the right thing in acquiring Subban.

Not only that, but then there was the question of Pekka Rinne—whose confidence seemingly had been completely shattered after a 5–0 loss to the San Jose Sharks in game seven of the Western Conference Semifinals back in May of that year.

They say time heals all wounds, but could Rinne and the Predators turn the page so quickly after another two-and-out the season before?

The Predators couldn't have asked for a better beginning to the new season, in a game against their old nemesis, the Chicago Blackhawks, at Bridgestone Arena.

It all began when Subban blistered home the first goal of the season for the Predators, en route to a 3–2 Predators win in the season opener.

It was the third-straight year that the Predators had won their season opener.

"I wanted to get my feet under me, play hard, and play physical and just try to do whatever the coaching staff asked me to do," Subban said to media after the game.

The home-opener, however, was some of the only good fortune the team would experience over the next handful of weeks.

Losing promptly in Chicago to the same Blackhawks team they had beaten the night before, Nashville lost again three nights later to the Dallas Stars back at home before heading up to Detroit for a meeting against the Red Wings.

Nashville prepared to face the Wings as it would against any opponent on the road: game-day skate, meet with the media, pregame meal, rest, and then game time.

After engaging in the typical pregame meal portion of the day, Nashville's players headed up to their rooms for rest before the 7:30 p.m. puck drop.

As players trickled into the arena hours before the start, Nashville's training staff became inundated with questions regarding nausea—seemingly foretelling the night that would come.

Just before the team hit the ice for pregame warm-ups, a smattering of players began to suddenly fall ill.

"Right before warmups, I started puking in the stalls there," said Johansen. "Then I went out for warmups, just trying to do everything I could to stay in the game, played the first period and I just couldn't move. And then I got in after the first period and I started puking uncontrollably."

Nashville had fallen victim to a suspected bout of food poisoning. Some players, like Johansen, found themselves unable to play, while others battled through it as the game continued.

Struggling already, the Predators lost to Detroit 5–3 before heading back to Nashville that night, in preparation for their matchup against the Pittsburgh Penguins less than 20 hours later.

"We were going down pretty hard," then-Predators forward James Neal said. "I've never seen that many guys get sick."

Some players for Nashville kept their bodies in check through the loss to the Red Wings, falling ill afterwards, during the flight back to Tennessee or sometime during the early morning hours.

Colton Sissons and Craig Smith were guaranteed scratches for the game against Pittsburgh. Pekka Rinne, who overcame fits of nausea to finish the game against Detroit, would be out as well against Detroit. Juuse Saros started and Marek Mazanec backed him up, and retired goaltender Chris Mason, Nashville's television color analyst, brought his equipment to the arena in the event that he were to be needed under emergency circumstances.

Predators captain Mike Fisher fell ill as well, starting to experience symptoms when the team landed back in Tennessee around 1 a.m. Central time.

"I was throwing up, and I couldn't keep anything in," Fisher said to reporters. "It's tough when you can't eat and then to try and play, then you're dehydrated."

With 20 percent of their active roster unable to play that evening, Poile did the only thing he could do: call in reinforcements from the Milwaukee Admirals.

Milwaukee had a game of their own Saturday night in Rockford against the IceHogs, but a contingent of Admirals players flew to Tennessee that morning from Wisconsin, diverting through Chicago—where forward Harry Zolnierczyk met them—and arriving in Nashville with time to spare prior to the game that evening.

"We got into a situation where we suspect that we're dealing with some food poisoning in Detroit," Poile said to reporters that morning. "We've got a lot of guys that are sick right now. Everything was fine yesterday, and it all happened just before and then during the game and after the game and it's continuing today.

"I've never been through this whole thing. The fact that there were seven or eight guys that had it, they gutted it out and they played and that's how we got 20 players in the lineup that night."

Altogether, Sissons, Smith, Rinne, Fisher, and Cody Bass were out of the lineup that evening for the Predators. Zolnierczyk, Austin Watson, Frederick Gaudreau, and Trevor Smith took their place.

It was a perfect storm for Nashville. They had lost their three previous games going into a game against the defending Stanley Cup champions with a depleted roster and several AHL players filling in.

Like the Predators somehow find a way to do, though, they handed a team they seemingly always struggle with a 5–1 loss despite all the adversity they had to overcome.

Nashville had an early-season moment of resiliency, one that helped shape the rest of the season. It also showed that the Predators, even when facing an up-hill battle from time to time, can be incredibly laid back as well.

The highlight of the whole food poisoning ordeal would come the morning prior to the game against the

Mike Fisher, who played his final 429 games with Nashville, was instrumental in leading the Predators to the Stanley Cup Final in 2017.

Penguins, when head coach Peter Laviolette showed his lighter side during a tough moment early in the season.

"Nobody wants to talk hockey? Just want to talk throw-up and diarrhea?"

As funny as the comment was, Nashville wouldn't have much to laugh about during the first month of the season.

Outside of the win over Pittsburgh, the Predators were mired in a slump, losing 8 of the first 11 games. After losing back-to-back games in the shootout during the first week of November, a switch seemed to flip somewhere for the team.

"It's concerning where we're at," Laviolette said to reporters after a 3–2 shootout loss to the Carolina Hurricanes on November 5th. "It's concerning with the inconsistency. It's not good enough. That's the bottom line.

"We weren't competitive enough. We weren't fast enough. Why? I don't know why."

The loss to Carolina would be one of the few Nashville would experience that month, ramping things up against their competition immediately afterwards.

A three-game winning streak at home would put the Predators back on track, pushing their record over .500 for the first time since opening night against Chicago.

"I think every year the seats get rearranged a little bit on the boat and you've got to figure out where your seat is and what's expected of you," said Laviolette to the media after a November 12th 5–0 blowout of the Anaheim Ducks. "There's definitely a little transition that we went through. I wish we handled it a little better and didn't get into that spot, but I think guys are scoring goals, too, now and they're getting a little bit of confidence on the ice."

Again, though, Nashville fell into another pattern of losing, seeing the team go through the entire month of December with five wins in 14 games—a far cry from going 9–3–2 the month before.

Harking back to their experiences one month prior, the Predators again had to battle through adversity.

Falling behind 3–0 to the St. Louis Blues early in the second period of a December 13th game, Nashville was well on its way to a third-straight loss and fifth in its past six games.

"Once they scored that third one, a nice pass on the power play and a good finish, we took off," said Johansen during his postgame media scrum. "Something triggered for us, and we were unstoppable."

Less than five minutes later, Neal and Filip Forsberg started the comeback for Nashville, scoring three minutes apart and cutting the Blues lead down to 3–2 entering the third period.

It wouldn't take long for the Predators to tie it up after that, as Johansen collected an errant puck on a delayed penalty to tie the game just three minutes into the final frame.

A goal from Mike Fisher and two from Mike Ribeiro cemented a 6–3 Nashville win, all six goals unanswered by the Blues.

"That's the best I've seen this team play," Johansen said after the win. "I think, since I've been here, just skating and everyone on the same page. You go through our whole lineup and everybody was doing so many great things out there. I think we really needed that win.

"We needed a character comeback win like that, and hopefully we'll be able to use that moving forward now for some confidence and knowing that we're always in a game."

On December 30th, less than three weeks after Nashville's comeback win, the Predators yet again used

St. Louis as a focal point for another milestone: Juuse Saros's first career shutout victory.

Dropping three of the next four afterwards, one a 2–1 overtime loss to Shea Weber and the visiting Montreal Canadiens on January 3rd, the Predators needed another dose of theatrics to turn things around for them during the first weeks of 2017.

Historically, Nashville hasn't been the most successful of teams in overtime since the league switched from a four-on-four format to a three-on-three format. Two wins in 18 trips to overtime—not including any games that went to a shootout—since the league switched to that format prior to the 2015–16 season wasn't what Nashville had had in mine.

They had the talent. They had the defense. They had the goaltending. Yet, for whatever reason, the Predators simply couldn't win many games during the five-minute period between a tied game ending in regulation and a coin-flip shootout.

Against the visiting Canucks in early January, Nashville found itself heading to overtime after a Brandon Sutter goal with 49 seconds left in regulation tied the game at one.

It almost felt like a given at that point: either the Predators were going to lose at some point in overtime or, if things went their way in the shootout, maybe they could collect that second point.

Just 20 seconds in, Nashville looked as though they had won the game. Roman Josi launched a shot bar-down past goaltender Ryan Miller and a leaping Viktor Arvidsson.

Immediately waved off by the referee, a review showed contact between Arvidsson and Miller. Overtime again looked to be Nashville's crux.

The Canucks ended up spending the final 1:40 of the overtime period on a power play, just another nail in the coffin for the Predators' hopes to somehow manage a victory. Yet, as the final seconds ticked off the clock, Nashville got one final opportunity.

After blocking a shot, Roman Josi and Calle Jarnkrok found themselves cruising toward Miller with just five seconds to go as they passed the blue line into the offensive zone.

Josi quickly passed the puck onto Jarnkrok's stick, and Jarnkrock in turn roofed it past Miller, giving Nashville its third win in 19 trips to overtime. All with 1.5 seconds left on the clock.

"We just knew we had to stick with it," said forward Austin Watson postgame, who scored Nashville's lone regulation goal in the second period. "There's only two ways to go about it: You either keep working or you just kind of give up, and we're not going to do that. We had to battle and find a way. It's kind of fitting that it ended that way."

That game symbolized the start of a 9–3–1 stretch for Nashville, pushing the record on the season to 26–19–8 by February 7th and the Predators into the top three of the Central Division.

Yet if it weren't for an incredible personal performance from forward Filip Forsberg two weeks later, the Predators may have found themselves wrapped up in another losing streak—no telling the full extent of it.

Since the last week of January, Forsberg couldn't find the back of the net.

Scoring 7 goals in the first 12 games of the new calendar year, Forsberg's Midas-like touch had gone cold—collecting only one goal in 10 games between January 25th and February 20th.

As Forsberg goes, seemingly so do the Predators. During his slump, they couldn't post better than a 5–5–0 record—treading water in the league's most difficult division while their rivals climbed past them.

to the players and coaches next time I see them in the locker room.

Which I don't and, from the advice he's given me to pass along, it's probably a good thing I haven't.

We're fortunate in Nashville to have multiple professional sports teams. It gives those of us who love sports an outlet to watch and celebrate our teams on a weekly or, in the case of sports outside the NFL, daily basis. It also gives those who *aren't* sports fans a chance to become one. I can't tell you the number of times I've spoken to fans who are attending their first Predators game or who are bringing their kid for their first time or are still trying to grasp and understand all the rules, starting conversations with, "this may seem like a stupid question. . ."

There are no stupid questions when it comes to learning a sport. There never will be.

Everybody has their own stories regarding how they became a fan. There isn't an exception, just another story to be added to the book. Luckily, when it comes to the Nashville Predators and one of the most loyal and dedicated fanbases I've ever seen, not to mention *loud*, there are plenty of stories yet to be written.

The 2018–19 season will mark the twentieth year of hockey in the city of Nashville. It may be a far cry from the 100th anniversary the Montreal Canadiens celebrated recently, but fortunately Nashville is unlike any other city in the world.

When hockey can thrive in such a non-traditional market like Nashville, you know there must be something special about it. And anyone who's visited to take in a Predators game will tell you that's 100 percent accurate.

Filip Forsberg, who was traded to Nashville in 2013, recorded a franchise-high 16 points during the postseason run of 2017.

He's one of the Predators' most legitimate scoring threats they've had in franchise history.

Climbing back from a 4–1 deficit against the Flames on February 21st, Forsberg netted three of the next four

goals for Nashville—all coming in the second period over a span of 8:37 to give Nashville a 5–4 lead.

While the Predators ultimately dropped the game 6–5 in overtime, it was an incredible individual effort for Forsberg.

No one thought he could duplicate the feat two days later.

Again, finding a way to help Nashville battle back from a deficit, Forsberg recorded a natural hat trick with two goals in the second and one 37 seconds to begin the third period. He became the first person to record back-to-back hat tricks in the NHL since Canucks forward Alexandre Burrows accomplished the same feat on January 5 and 7, 2010.

"I think I always felt a responsibility, and I think that goes for every player in this locker room," Forsberg said to reporters after the game. "Everyone wants to contribute and help the team win. Obviously I can't expect myself to score a hat trick every game, but I just try to work hard and if I can score goals, I'll take that as well."

It would be the start of a four-game winning streak, followed by a four-game losing streak and then a 7–1–0 stretch—bringing the Predators' record to 39–25–11 on March 27th and, again, placing them third in the division—only one point ahead of the Blues, having played the same number of games.

Unfortunately for Nashville, they wouldn't be able to lock down a spot among the division's top three to guarantee a place in the playoffs. Instead, the Predators would fall to the second wildcard spot in the Western Conference, matching them in the first round against a team with whom they had plenty of history—the Chicago Blackhawks.

Having been dispatched by Chicago in six games in both previous playoffs, Nashville hoped to accept a different fate in 2017. This time, with the Predators squeaking

into the playoffs again by the skin of their teeth, nobody gave them any chance to escape past the first round, many predicting a Blackhawks sweep or a five-game loss for Nashville.

The experts had made it known that Nashville didn't stand much of a chance.

That, however, is the beauty of the Predators— they've never cared much for the outside noise. Not many teams allow that from the outside to impact their locker room, yet it served as bulletin board material for Nashville.

Coming into game one against Chicago, the Predators had dropped 9 of their previous 10 inside the United Center.

With a first-period goal from Viktor Arvidsson and a 29-save shutout from Pekka Rinne, the Predators started the playoffs with a 1–0 win. Improbable at best, it put home-ice advantage back in the hands of the Predators with a likely split against Chicago after game two.

Yet Nashville had incredibly different plans than everyone else.

Sixty minutes, 5 goals, 30 saves, and another shutout for Rinne later, the Predators held a 2–0 series lead—the second time in franchise history that they had ever led 2–0 against a team in the playoffs, doing so against the Ducks one year prior before dropping the next three and winning in seven. It was only the fifth time in NHL history at that point that a team started a playoff series on the road with two straight shut-outs.

"That wasn't the game plan coming in here, to leave here and say, 'Oh yeah, they'll get nothing.' But our guys went to work and did a good job," said Laviolette to media after game two.

Game three wouldn't be more of the same for Nashville. In fact, they would trail for the first time this

series, a two-goal deficit after two periods they'd have to find an answer for if they wanted to push the Blackhawks to the brink of elimination.

Less than three minutes into the third, Rinne would be put to the test—having to come up big against Chicago's Nick Schmaltz on a breakaway. If converted, it would have put Nashville down 3–0 and, likely, produced a much different result for the series overall.

Forsberg was instrumental to the Predators during the 2017 season and continues to be one of Nashville's most lethal goal-scorers.

"At the time, that was probably the most critical point in the game at 2–0 and a breakaway coming down," Laviolette continued. "If you want to know where the game kind of clicked for us into our favor, it was that save right there by [Rinne]."

Just two minutes after the failed breakaway, Nashville got on the board. Filip Forsberg's mid-air batting of the puck past Corey Crawford halved Chicago's 2–0 lead.

Ten minutes later, Forsberg tied the game at two. Although it was only the first round of the playoffs, these were the early signs of a team that was benefitting from the right calls, bounces, and momentum shifts.

Those are the little pieces of the puzzle that make champions in the NHL.

Again, Predators players were in the right place at the right time against a Blackhawks team that was one goal away from being down 3–0 in the series.

Kevin Fiala made it so, taking a James Neal pass in the slot, pulling Crawford out of his net, and sliding it past him in overtime.

Nashville was now one game away from a four-game sweep of Chicago—something no expert could, or would have, predicted.

"It's just character," said Fiala during his postgame scrum after his overtime winner. "When we went in [to the locker room] before the third period, we could feel it. We were going to do it. Everybody believed in it. Everybody was just working hard from the first and last guy, and that's why we did it."

Three days later, in front of another sold-out crowd at Bridgestone Arena, the Predators wrote their own history.

With a 1–0 lead entering the third period, Nashville went up 3–0 thanks to a goal by Colton Sissons and Josi's second of the night before Arvidsson would close the deal

with 1:48 remaining to give the Predators a 4–1 victory over the Blackhawks.

It was their first sweep in franchise history and the first time a number one-seeded team had been swept by a number eight-seeded team in NHL history.

"We're only concerned about one thing right now, honestly," said Predators captain Mike Fisher to media after game four. "Guys played some great hockey. There's so much belief in our room, really. We believed we could beat that team. I don't think hardly anyone else did, but that didn't matter. Now it's just what's next, focusing on that, and just keep getting better through these playoffs and worry about that next team."

It wouldn't get any easier after that for the Predators; they would still have to make their way past another member of the Central Division before the Western Conference Finals. To date, the Preds had never been outside of the second round and whoever they were to face next would be a first-time playoff opponent for them.

Two days after Nashville's sweep, the Blues finished off a five-game drubbing of the Minnesota Wild to make their way into the second round—pitting two teams 300 miles apart against each other for the first time in the Stanley Cup Playoffs.

Nashville had already won the season series against St. Louis. As long-time divisional rivals meeting for the first time, both teams knew it would be a tough, physical series with a spot in the Conference Final on the line.

The Blues had been in the Conference Final three times previously, the last being a six-game loss to the Sharks in 2016. But, much as the Predators luck had been, St. Louis largely couldn't find their way out of the second round, losing in either the first or second round in their last eight trips to the playoffs before 2016.

The year 2001 was the last time before that where St. Louis had been to the third round, sending the Avalanche on their way to the Stanley Cup Final after five games.

Relishing the opportunity, the Predators continued in game one right where they left off against the Blackhawks, tallying the opening goal and holding St. Louis off the board for a 1–0 lead after 20 minutes.

Then, disaster struck.

Speeding into the Blues zone, Kevin Fiala collected a loose puck and tried to drive toward Blues goaltender Jake Allen. Attempting to turn and continue the play around the back of the net, Fiala was driven straight into the boards, at high speed, by St. Louis defenseman Robert Bortuzzo.

Fiala suffered a fractured left femur on the play, having to be carried off on a stretcher and taken to a local hospital for surgery. He wouldn't return that season.

It was a monumental loss for the Predators, who were finally seeing Fiala bud into a legitimate scoring threat. For Nashville, though, there wasn't anything anyone could do but play on.

"It was tough," said Subban after the game. "You never want to see a young kid go down like that and be taken off on a stretcher. I've experienced it before and it's not fun, especially for your family and friends, so we hope he's OK."

After going up 3–1 by the end of the second period, the Predators had only 20 minutes left to win their fifth straight game of the playoffs. In a span of 2:34 midway through the third, however, the game would be tied.

Enter Vernon Fiddler.

Early in February, Nashville made a small trade to bring back Fiddler for the stretch run. Fiddler had spent the first six seasons of his career with the Predators before playing for Phoenix, Dallas, and New Jersey.

Statistically, his return to Nashville hadn't been the greatest, as Fiddler scored just one goal in the remaining 20 games of the regular season after his trade. He'd also record only two points throughout the entire playoff run for the Predators, one goal and one assist.

But his goal couldn't have been a timelier one.

As time dwindled down during a tied game one between the Predators and Blues, Austin Watson attempted to drive the puck into the offensive zone, only to have it deflected off his stick by forward Ryan Reeves.

Unfortunately for Reeves, the puck still careened into the offensive zone.

Blues defenseman Jay Bouwmeester tried to knock the puck back and out, only to have it bounce off Watson, straight to his stick. Watson then slid it to an open Fiddler 10 feet in front of him.

As the puck bounced around Fiddler's feet, the journeyman forward swatted it toward the net, watching it flutter through the five-hole of a diving Allen and into the net.

The Predators had just taken a 4–3 lead with five minutes to go on what would be a game-winning goal from Fiddler.

"It was just a quick transition," Fiddler said about his goal. "I saw Watson kind of get it in his feet outside and just tried to get to the net. He made a little flip pass and I just got a piece of it and just chipped it over the goalie. Lucky one."

Securing home-ice back in its favor for the second series in a row, Nashville settled for a split in the first two contests before heading back to the Music City for games three and four—a chance to capitalize on the hard work displayed back in the opener of the series.

Up one goal heading into the second period, the Predators again would benefit from a lucky bounce of the

puck, something that was becoming a trend during this run for Nashville.

Ekholm dished a cross-ice pass through the neutral zone to Sissons, who lobbed the puck to Cody McLeod— the most unlikely of targets—who was streaming down the slot.

Deflecting the puck in the air while on its course, McLeod forced Allen to make a split-second save, producing a rebound behind the net which McLeod would angle past Allen for a 2–0 Predators lead.

"I just tried to send it back to the net and create a scramble," McLeod told reporters after the game. "Luckily it bounced in."

St. Louis got one back before the end of the period, yet it wasn't enough, and the Preds took a 2–1 lead in the series over the Blues.

Both games four and five showcased goaltending and defensive efforts over offensive prowess, with Rinne posting 32 saves in a 2–1 win in game four—giving the Predators a 3–1 series lead. Allen staved off elimination in game five with a 21-save performance to cut Nashville's lead to 3–2.

Six games ended up being enough for the Predators.

Breaking a 1–1 tie less than four minutes into the third period, Johansen took an Arvidsson feed and deked past Allen into the net to push the Predators in front 2–1. What made that goal particularly spectacular was the fact that defenseman Yannick Weber had given Johansen a slight push with his stick, boosting Johansen through the neutral zone and putting him in place to be able to receive Arvidsson's cross-ice pass.

"What a pass by [Arvidsson]," said Johansen to the media afterwards. "I don't know if you guys noticed, but Yannick Weber with the sense of mind to push me from behind to give me a little boost got me in a position

where I could be in alone with the goalie. Huge credit to [Weber]."

They would need to hold St. Louis for nearly 17 minutes to move on.

As the Blues tried to counter, Nashville pressed. Wave after wave, opportunity after opportunity, the Predators continued their attack.

Forsberg found himself on a breakaway three minutes after Johansen's tie-breaking goal, only to be denied by Allen.

The emotions on the ice, on the Predators bench, and in the stands was palpable. It no longer felt as if Nashville had to simply hold off the Blues, but rather, if they could add an insurance goal to their total, they'd seal the deal.

And then came Jarnkrok's empty-net goal with one minute left on the clock, indicating that Nashville would be heading to the Western Conference Final against the Anaheim Ducks.

"Right now it means everything," Rinne said to the media after the series win. "We haven't gone further than this before. It's a great feeling, but there's a lot of work left. After this second round, there's only four teams left. We all know we have what it takes, and everything is in our hands."

Only one team—a team that the Predators knew intimately in the playoffs—stood in Nashville's way of a trip to the Stanley Cup Final. It was a team they had faced and beaten in 2011 (six games) and 2016 (seven games): the Anaheim Ducks.

Game one was pivotal for both teams. In their history with the Ducks, the Predators had yet to lose a postseason game one—all three starting on the road.

Unlike their previous two starts against the Blackhawks and Blues, Nashville had to fight its way back from an early deficit.

Jakob Silfverberg's tally five minutes into the first period gave Anaheim a 1–0 lead. Forsberg, with a tip off an Irwin shot from the point, answered seven minutes later to make it 1–1.

Austin Watson's one-timer off a Johansen pass early in the third gave Nashville a 2–1 lead they held through 40 minutes of play.

Going into the third period, both teams knew exactly what was at stake. The Predators could again swing home-ice back in their favor with a series-opening win at Anaheim while the Ducks, conversely, could put Nashville in a position they had yet to be all postseason long: trailing a series.

Seven minutes, 21 seconds into the third, Anaheim defenseman Hampus Lindholm sent a shot screaming through traffic past Rinne to tie the game at two.

It took overtime to decide what had turned out to be a thrilling start to the Western Conference Final—Nashville's second overtime game of the playoffs and Anaheim's fourth to that point.

Tightly contested with attacks on both sides of the ice, it was the Predators' toughest matchup to date. Both teams knew the other's tendencies. Both knew how to exploit the other's goaltender. Both equally had burrowed under the skin of the other.

Whether it was four, five, six, or seven games, it was going to be nasty and drawn-out between the two.

Yet, Nashville again found a way to break through in game one.

As the Predators circled through the Ducks zone, Ekholm started a fantastic scoring chance down-low by sweeping into the slot, only to have the puck deflected away while nine of the ten players on the ice swarmed around Ducks goaltender John Gibson.

The puck found its way behind Gibson's net, where Ekholm would pass it back to Subban at the point and then over to Neal, who blasted a shot off the head of a diving Corey Perry and past Gibson for the overtime winner.

Nashville again had won the first game of the series. They again had swung home-ice back in their favor. Most importantly, they were now only three wins away from a trip to the Stanley Cup Final.

Ten minutes into the first period of game two, the Predators had already grabbed a two-goal lead and were just 40 minutes away from heading back home up two games to nothing, attempting to repeat the effort they had during the first round against Chicago.

Unlike its games against the Blackhawks, Anaheim had plenty left in its arsenal to combat the Predators. A two-goal lead, especially in the first period, isn't nearly enough to put away the Ducks even on their worst nights.

With one minute left in the first, Sami Vatanen converted a late power-play opportunity to bring Anaheim within one as the period closed. As momentum shifted heading to the second period, Jakob Silfverberg would make the most of it, tying the game just 39 seconds into the middle frame.

Against both Chicago and St. Louis, the Predators had never truly faced any adversity. It was clear that this series would be different, however, and how Nashville would respond would be key. Unfortunately in game two, their response wasn't enough to keep the Ducks at bay.

After Forsberg scored the go-ahead goal midway through the second, Anaheim rattled off three unanswered goals to shock the Preds and even the series at one game apiece. It also saw the Ducks begin a type of mind game with the Predators, in an effort to try and force Nashville into making silly mistakes.

Ryan Kesler, who arguably is one player fans around the league—outside of the team he plays for—dislike the most, continued to draw the ire of Nashville, especially that of Johansen. After game two, Johansen made it a point to call Kesler out during his media scrum.

"I mean, it just blows my mind watching," Johansen said to media after game two. "I don't know what's going through his head over there. Like his family and his friends watching him play, I don't know how you cheer for a guy like that. It just doesn't make sense how he plays the game. I'm just trying to go out there and play hockey, and it sucks when you've got to pull a stick out of your groin every shift."

Even with Johansen's pointed commentary, it didn't shift the focus from what had already happened. Anaheim had tied up the series in game two, yet play was set to resume back in Nashville after the split.

Heading back home for two games gave Nashville a chance to put a stranglehold on the Ducks—much like they had done for both Chicago and St. Louis leading to the Western Conference Final.

Nashville got the start they needed, winning game three 2–1 and jumping ahead in the series by the same margin.

Again, the Predators in that game had to come from behind to win against Anaheim, much like they did in game one.

As dominant as they'd been through the first two rounds of the playoffs, some of the steam had slowly been leaking from the Preds' playoff war machine. Anaheim had found ways to expose the Predators on the ice, but not a way to knock them down for good.

Nashville still had plenty of fight left. They had the series lead and home-ice still in their favor. And with six straight wins on home ice to start the playoffs behind

them, they'd look for a seventh to allow them to secure a 3–1 series lead.

It would take a stroke of luck for a visiting team to win at Bridgestone Arena in the playoffs that season. For the Ducks, they'd take just that.

Seeing Nashville claw back from a 2–0 deficit in a six-minute span during the third period, including a goal from Forsberg in the final minute of regulation, Ducks forward Corey Perry—one of the few players that has singularly drawn the ire of fans in Nashville for many years—lobbed a puck toward the net midway through the first overtime period, deflecting off the stick of Subban and into the net.

The first bad bounce of the playoffs for Nashville had cost them an overtime game and the lead in the series.

That wasn't even the worst news of the night, either: Johansen was done for the rest of the playoffs as well as captain Mike Fisher for the series, the latter being diagnosed with a concussion in part due to an inadvertent knee to the head.

After being checked into the boards by Ducks defenseman Josh Manson during the second period of game four, Johansen was treated for acute compartment syndrome of the left thigh. Unaware of any injury during the game, Johansen finished the overtime loss in game four only to find himself with difficulty getting changed after the game, then unable to walk prior to leaving the arena.

"It happened pretty fast," Johansen told reporters. "I got off the ice and I was having a tough time just standing and getting my gear off, and then obviously I went right back to the medical guys on our team. First thing, looked at it, looks like it was going to be a charley horse, started swelling up, so started icing it and doing all that stuff, and then I was going to go shower and come back and put some wrap on it, and then get home and get some rest.

"By the time I walked to the shower, finished showering, and tried to get on my underwear, I couldn't walk. I had to get one of the guys to grab a trainer and come back and help me to the medical room. And then the docs looked at it again, and the swelling increased by like triple it seemed in those 20 minutes when I was walking around and getting ready to go home. It turned into pretty quick transition where I just needed to head over [to the hospital] and get it looked at and take the next step, I guess."

Without the services of Fiala, and now Johansen, Nashville would be without two of their top six forwards for the remainder of the playoffs. They'd needed another hero to step up.

For the Predators, heroes could come from anywhere.

Pontus Aberg, who had spent the majority of his season with the Admirals in Milwaukee before injuries pushed him up the depth chart, scored the game-winner in the final 10 minutes of regulation in game five to give the Predators a 3–2 lead in the series.

Colton Sissons, who started his career for Nashville playing for Trotz but truly began to thrive under Laviolette, scored Nashville's second-ever hat trick in the playoffs in a 6–3 win over Anaheim. In doing so, the Predators knocked the Ducks out for the third straight time they had faced them.

"I don't think I could have dreamt of this moment, scoring a hat trick in a Western Conference clinching game," said Sissons to the media afterwards. "I can't speak enough of our whole group. We've been through some challenges together, and we stuck together no matter what. We believed, and here we are."

Nashville, however, would begin to run out of steam.

Down its top center going into the Stanley Cup Final against the Penguins, Nashville had to rely on

Fisher (who wasn't at 100 percent), Sissons, Jarnkrok, and Gaudreau down the middle. Against players like Sidney Crosby, Evgeni Malkin, Nick Bonino, and former Predator Matt Cullen, it was a tall task.

If games one and two were any indication, it would be next-to-impossible.

After climbing back from a 3–0 deficit in the third period, the Predators succumbed to Pittsburgh in the opener of the Final 5–3, Nashville's first series-opening loss of the playoffs.

Things didn't get any better, as Nashville headed home for games three and four down 2–0 in the series after the Penguins blasted them 4–1 in game two.

All the home-ice magic the Preds had benefited from to this point would direly be needed if the Predators were going to hang around with the defending Stanley Cup Champions, who were now only two wins away from back-to-back Cups.

Rinne and the Predators allowed two goals total while on home ice, winning games three and four by a combined 9–2 score. Gaudreau—who didn't have a locker in the Preds' locker room during the Final—nevertheless scored a goal in each game.

"I could be sitting on the floor and I would take it," Gaudreau said. "I'm just happy to be here. I don't really care about the stall, to be honest."

The Predators could not seem to carry their momentum into game five against the defending champs.

Three goals spread out through the second period would put Nashville down 6–0 after 40 minutes—a score that would stand through the final period of play.

The Predators were 60 minutes from seeing their dreams slip through their fingers. After such an amazing season to get where they were, they'd have to find

a Herculean effort and take every ounce of energy from their fanbase to fight back against the Penguins.

Nashville's crowd had been there from the start, swelling to record numbers as the Predators traveled further and further into the postseason. By the Stanley Cup Final, the Walk of Fame Park—directly adjacent to Bridgestone Arena—had to be capped by city officials to guarantee some level of comfort to those who attended.

The overflow lined the streets near the arena. Fifth Avenue beside Bridgestone, Broadway from 3rd Avenue all the way back up to 5th, lining the rooftops of all the Honky Tonk bars that stretched through the downtown area, fans from all over came down to cheer on the Predators in their search for the city's first professional sports championship.

While the Tennessee Titans took Nashville and its growing base of sports fans to the Super Bowl in 1999, it had been nearly twenty years since the city had a chance to celebrate like it did then.

It was nearly impossible to maneuver through the streets of downtown the Sunday of game six. Fans, especially those without a ticket to the game, arrived hours upon hours in advance, just to secure a place outside of Bridgestone Arena to sit and watch the game on the giant television screens the Predators had set up.

Team officials estimated that 20,000 to 30,000 fans would make their way downtown to watch the game, in which Nashville was trying to tie the series up and force a Cup-deciding game seven.

After a scoreless opening twenty minutes, the Predators came out on fire trying to get the first score of the game in their favor. Speeding along the boards off to the left of Penguins goaltender Matt Murray, Sissons collected a turnover from Pittsburgh and sent it cross-ice

to a wide-open Aberg with the best chance of the game thus far.

Saved by Murray—a spectacular save to keep it scoreless.

Immediately off the shot, the puck rebounded off Murray's right leg straight to two battling players, where Aberg swept back in and re-collected the puck.

Passing it backwards, Aberg found Ekholm, who then dropped it off to Forsberg, screaming toward Murray with a perfect chance to capitalize on the confused Penguins.

Letting go of his shot, it found its way under the left arm of Murray and plopped onto the blue ice behind him. An opportunistic Sissons poked the puck in and gave Nashville a crucial 1–0 lead in a pivotal game six.

Or not.

Losing sight of the puck in the moments it was temporarily lodged between the arm and body of Murray, referee Kevin Pollock blew his whistle to stop play as he had lost track of the puck.

The entire process took less than two seconds of real time, from Forsberg firing the shot to Pollock blowing his whistle and finishing with Sissons poking the puck in. It happened so quickly nobody in the stands noticed it, but Predators players and coaches were furious.

The goal was called back and play moved on, the game remaining scoreless.

Time continued to tick off the clock as Nashville continued to get chances, all stopped by Murray. Sissons even had a couple additional opportunities himself, including a clean breakaway, but the Predators just couldn't solve Murray.

With under two minutes left in regulation, Pittsburgh drove the play back into Nashville's end. Circling the puck around the boards, Penguins defenseman Chris

Kunitz got the puck back to fellow defenseman Justin Schultz—who sent it wide to the left of Rinne.

A split-second later, former Predator and now Penguins forward Patric Hornqvist batted the puck as it bounced off the boards back toward the play out of mid-air, off the back of Rinne, and into the back of the net.

Every ounce of great luck Nashville had seen go in its favor over the last two months evaporated over the course of 60 minutes—from the goal called back due to the whistle being blown early to now seeing a longtime former Predators player score what appeared to be the Cup-winning goal banking it off Rinne and in.

Eighty-one seconds later, Carl Hagelin sent in the empty net goal that gave the Penguins a 2–0 lead and sealed their back-to-back championships.

"It's hard to describe," said Subban after the game. "You dream about lifting the Stanley Cup as a young kid, and the dream has happened probably a million times for most of us. Being that close, being two games away. . . it [stinks]. But for us, we did so many things well and this is such a tremendous run for our team, and we have such a young team. I think we gained a ton of experience from this run."

Nashville's season ended 61 minutes and 35 seconds from winning a Stanley Cup, a number that motivated them in the very next season, during which they won a franchise-first Central Division title and the team's first ever Presidents' Trophy. They ultimately fell to the Winnipeg Jets in game seven of the second round of the playoffs, a far cry from where they had ended just 11 months prior.

It was a tough blow for the Predators. Everything that had gone on from the start of the franchise—the ownership change, the team nearly being sold, countless play-off series loss after loss before finally breaking through,

just to get near the top of the mountain and knocked off before reaching the peak.

But losing the Stanley Cup Finals provided a great lesson for Nashville, one that continues to stick with the players and coaches that remain from that run.

Predators fans got a true taste of what greatness feels like. Even with the team coming up just short, it was arguably the greatest moment in franchise history—only to be topped by one day in the future, on which Nashville will hopefully hoist the Stanley Cup for itself.

Chapter Seventeen

Final Note

My father played a pivotal role in creating the sports junkie that I am today. I honestly wouldn't be where I am now, had it not been for the numerous contacts and friendships he gained throughout the years, which seemed to enable him to always find himself with a set of four tickets to each Predators game, even though we weren't season ticket holders.

I didn't start writing about the Predators until 2011; until then I was strictly a fan. For nine years prior to that, I went to nearly every game. It was easy to get tickets back then, especially if you knew someone who worked in the building or for the team itself. Comps were everywhere, and that's not a slight at the team, just a truth.

There was a time when my brother, my dad, and I had the same routine every single game: park for free near the Southern Baptist Convention building at the corner of 8th Avenue and Commerce Street (which you can no longer do, as it's become a pay lot), walk three blocks down to Broadway to eat dinner at Samboni's Pizza, then go and watch some hockey.

Samboni's isn't something a lot of you will remember, but for a time it was arguably Nashville's best pizza place. Now, a familiar pizza place—Mellow Mushroom—sits in its place.

But we'd take in nearly every game, every season, on Tuesdays, Thursdays, and Saturdays, with other scattered days of the week thrown in from time to time. When the building would have 12,000 fans in it and when there wasn't a seat left, we were there.

Dad has his faults, as we all do, and no matter how many times we ever disagreed, one thing that always brought us together were hockey games. Though I made a point of not talking too much in the car ride home after losses, because he took them a little harder than most and reasoning with someone like my father is quite an impossible task.

From our love of hockey grew an inseparable bond. After I graduated college, got married, and moved out, I'd still call my dad during and after games, as we'd dissect certain plays, how goals were scored, and the occasional berating of the officials.

His love of hockey helped mold me into the writer I became.

Now, stricken with Alzheimer's, he doesn't remember much about the games that we may have went to back when I was younger, wasn't married, and didn't have kids—before I started writing about the sport we love. That hasn't stopped him from watching every single Predators game that comes on television, which happens to be all of them these days.

It also doesn't stop us from talking about their games, like we used to. I don't have a chance to call him as much during or after games anymore, but typically the next day I'll call to make sure he was watching and, like he always does, he'll pass along his advice for me to give